Alastair
Sawday's

Special Places
to Stay

Paris

First edition
Copyright © 2009 Alastair Sawday
Publishing Co. Ltd

Published in September 2009

Alastair Sawday Publishing Co. Ltd,
The Old Farmyard, Yanley Lane,
Long Ashton, Bristol BS41 9LR, UK
Tel: +44 (0)1275 395430
Fax: +44 (0)1275 393388
Email: info@sawdays.co.uk
Web: www.sawdays.co.uk

The Globe Pequot Press,
P. O. Box 480, Guilford,
Connecticut 06437, USA
Tel: +1 203 458 4500
Fax: +1 203 458 4601
Email: info@globepequot.com
Web: www.globepequot.com

Maps: Maidenhead Cartographic Services
Printing: Butler Tanner & Dennis, Frome
UK distribution: Penguin UK, London

ISBN-13: 978-1-906136-21-5

Contents

Photo: www.istock.com

The buildings

Beautiful as they were, our old offices leaked heat, used electricity to heat water and rooms, flooded spaces with light to illuminate one person, and were not ours to alter. So in 2005 we created our own eco-offices by converting some old barns to create a low-emissions building. We made the building energy-efficient through a variety of innovative and energy-saving building techniques, described below.

Insulation We went to great lengths to ensure that very little heat will escape, by:
• laying insulating board 90mm thick immediately under the roof tiles and on the floor
• lining the whole of the inside of the building with plastic sheeting to ensure air-tightness
• fixing further insulation underneath the roof and between the rafters
• fixing insulated plaster-board to add yet another layer of insulation.
All this means we are insulated for the Arctic, and almost totally air-tight.

Heating We installed a wood-pellet boiler from Austria, in order to be largely fossil-fuel free. The pellets are made from compressed sawdust, a waste product from timber mills that work only with sustainably managed forests. The heat is conveyed by water, throughout the building, via an under-floor system.

Water We installed a 6000-litre tank to collect rainwater from the roofs. This is pumped back, via an ultra-violet filter, to the lavatories, showers and basins. There are two solar thermal panels on the roof providing heat to the one (massively insulated) hot-water cylinder.

Lighting We have a carefully planned mix of low-energy lighting: task lighting and up-lighting. We also installed three sun-pipes — polished aluminium tubes that reflect the outside light down to chosen areas of the building.

Electricity All our electricity has long come from the Good Energy company and is 100% renewable.

Materials Virtually all materials are non-toxic or natural. Our carpets, for example, are made from (80%)

Photo: Tom Germain

Herdwick sheep-wool from National Trust farms in the Lake District.

Doors and windows Outside doors and new windows are wooden, double-glazed and beautifully constructed in Norway. Old windows have been double-glazed.

We have a building we are proud of, and architects and designers are fascinated by. But best of all, we are now in a better position to encourage our owners and readers to take sustainability more seriously.

What we do

Besides having moved the business to a low-carbon building, the company works in a number of ways to reduce its overall environmental footprint.

Our footprint We measure our footprint annually and use this information to find ways of reducing our environmental impact. To help address unavoidable carbon emissions we try to put something back: since 2006 we have supported SCAD, an organisation that works with villagers in India to create genuinely sustainable development.

Our office Nearly all of our office waste is recycled; kitchen waste is composted and used in the office vegetable garden. Left-over fruit and veg goes to the locally-owned pigs across the lane, who have recently been joined by chickens rescued from battery farms. Organic and fairtrade basic provisions are used in the staff kitchen and at in-house events, and green cleaning products are used throughout the office.

For many years Alastair Sawday Publishing has been 'greening' the business in different ways. Our aim is to reduce our environmental footprint as far as possible, and almost every decision we make takes into account the environmental implications. In recognition of our efforts we won a Business Commitment to the Environment Award in 2005, and in 2006 a Queen's Award for Enterprise in the Sustainable Development category. In that year Alastair was voted ITN's 'Eco Hero'. In 2009 we were given the South West C+ Carbon Positive Consumer Choices Award for our Ethical Collection.

In 2008 and again in 2009 we won the IPG Environmental Award. In 2009 we were also the IPG overall Independent Publisher and Trade Publisher of the Year. The judging panel were effusive in their praise, stating: "With green issues currently at the forefront of publishers' minds, Alastair Sawday Publishing was singled out in this category as a model for all independents to follow. Its efforts to reduce waste in its office and supply chain have reduced the company's environmental impact, and it works closely with staff to identify more areas of improvement. Here is a publisher who lives and breathes green. Alastair Sawday has all the right principles and is clearly committed to improving its practice further."

We don't plan to pursue growth for growth's sake. The Sawday's name – and thus our future – depends on maintaining our integrity. We promote special places – those that add beauty, authenticity and a touch of humanity to our lives. This is a niche, albeit a growing one, so we will spend time pursuing truly special places rather than chasing the mass market.

That said, we do plan to produce more titles as well as to diversify. We are explanding our Go Slow series and have published *Green Europe*, both projects designed to raise the profile of low-impact tourism. Our Fragile Earth imprint is a growing collection of campaigning books about the environment that will keep you up to date and well-armed for the battle with apathy.

Paris has brilliantly resisted the sort of change that has almost ruined so many other lovely cities. Is it just because there has been a firm and clear policy about – among other things – the Paris skyline? Or is it a sophisticated mix of mayoral ambition and flair, conservatism, pride and bloody-mindedness?

For many of the same reasons we have made this book as beautiful and rewarding as we can. The Paris corner of our website attracts more visitors than almost any other, and for this book we have stretched the very notion of 'Paris' and taken you to the outskirts and beyond, to Versailles in the west and Picardy in the north. We haven't confined ourselves to hotels either; we introduce you to B&Bs, flats and apartments – anywhere beautiful and convivial to stay.

The result is a very engaging guide to how to make the most of your time in Paris. We don't tell you where to shop, to browse, to learn and to relax; we hope that the people you stay with can do that. In our long experience they do it with warmth and panache.

Photo: Tom Germain

If, by the way, you have not yet tried the remarkable Vélib' bike system, do! I recently arrived at the Gare du Nord with three cases and somehow managed to pedal my way across Paris to the Gare du Lyon. The bike stood the strain, and so did I. In fact, the journey was entertaining and safe, most of it along protected cycle lanes. Cars and other cyclists kept clear – perhaps no surprise. On another occasion I had a spare hour and used a bike to reach the Canal St Martin for a delightful ride along its banks. The 'lib' part is so true: the system lends a form of freedom to Parisians and visitors alike.

Do remember, when you are planning your Paris trip, that the rail system puts the city at the heart of a spider's web of fascinating places to visit. It is only a short ride to deep countryside. Or you can be in St Denis, admiring its stupendous cathedral, Tours to wander in a beautiful city and even see some châteaux. Rouen is some distance away by car but very close by rail, much of it along the Seine. It is a city of huge riches, a cathedral and massive churches, mediaeval streets to explore and fine Normandy food to eat. The journey to and from Paris is, for many, a quick commute.

So your Paris stay can be richer than you might have imagined. Nowadays there is little reason to be confined to the tourist districts and sights. There is much, much more and it is so easy to discover. Ask the owners of these special places; they are ready to be your Paris friends.

Alastair Sawday

Photo left: Le Logis d'Arnières, entry 102
Photo right: Le Sainte Beuve, entry 31

It's simple. There are no rules, no boxes to tick. We choose places that we like and are fiercely subjective in our choices. We also recognise that one person's idea of special is not necessarily someone else's so we try to give a variety of places, and prices. We take huge pleasure in finding people and places that do their own thing, brilliantly; places that are unusual and follow no trends; places of peace and beauty; people who are kind and interesting – and genuine.

Remember that the owners are experts at knowing their patch. They can often recommend sights to see, excellent restaurants, and gardens to visit.

Inspections

We visit every place to get a feel for how it ticks. We don't take a clipboard and we don't have a list of what is acceptable and what is not. Instead, we chat for an hour or so with the owner or manager and look round. It's all very informal, but it gives us an excellent idea of who would enjoy staying there. If the visit happens to be the last of the day, we sometimes stay the night. Places are then revisited regularly so that we can keep things fresh and accurate.

Feedback

In between inspections we rely on feedback from our readers, as well as from staff members who are encouraged to visit places across the series. This feedback is invaluable to us and we always follow up on comments. We like your recommendations, too,

Photo left: Cazaudehore – La Forestière, entry 109
Photo right: Hôtel Louis II, entry 40

so please stay in touch and tell us about your experiences and your discoveries. You can use the feedback form in this book (page 153) or on our website (www.sawdays.co.uk).

Occasionally misunderstandings occur, even with the best of intentions. So if your bedroom is cold or the bedside light is broken, please don't seethe silently and write to us a week later. Say something to the owners at the time – they will be keen to put things right if they can.

Subscriptions

Owners pay to appear in our guides. Their fees go towards the high costs of inspecting, of producing an all-colour book and of maintaining our website. We only include places and owners that we find positively special;

it is not possible for anyone to buy their way into our guides, or to write their own descriptions.

Disclaimer

We make no claims to pure objectivity in choosing our Special Places. They are here because we like them. Our opinions and tastes are ours alone and this book is a statement of them; we hope that you will share them. We have done our utmost to get our facts right but apologise unreservedly for any mistakes that may have crept in.

You should know that we do not check such things as fire alarms, swimming pool security or any other regulation with which owners of properties receiving paying guests should comply. This is the responsibility of the owners.

Photo: Entry 22

Finding the right place for you

All these places are special in one way or another. All have been visited and then written about honestly so that you can decide for yourselves which will suit you. We all have different priorities, so do read the descriptions carefully and pick out the places where you will be comfortable. If something is particularly important to you then check when you book: a simple question or two can avoid misunderstandings.

Wherever you choose to stay, remember that the owners are experts at knowing their patch. They can often recommend sights to see, excellent restaurants, and gardens to visit – occasionally ones that aren't usually open to the public. Some places may provide maps of the city and a bus timetable. Do ask.

On the B&B pages you will find a variety of places, and also owners: some will be hovering with freshly baked cake when you arrive, others may be out shopping for your supper, having left a key under a stone. Mostly these are people's homes; you will encounter family life and its attendant chaos in some, and complete privacy in others, while a fair number of owners will be happy for you to stay all day.

We take huge pleasure in finding people and places that do their own thing, brilliantly; places that are unusual and follow no trends; places of peace and beauty; people who are kind and interesting – and genuine.

For those who prefer more anonymity, there are many wonderful hotels, some child-friendly, others more suited to those who prefer peace and quiet. A sprinkling of deeply spoiling hotels will keep the fashionistas happy, while there are family-run and comfortingly old-fashioned places for traditionalists. There are also some gorgeous self-catering places, some classically contemporary, a few crisply chic, others simple but cosy.

Maps

Each property is flagged with its entry number on the maps at the front. These maps are the best start to planning your trip, but you'll need a proper map of the city for real navigation. Most places will send you detailed instructions once you have booked your stay.

Photo left: Hôtel Pergolèse, entry 72
Photo right: L'Appart de la Folie-Méricourt, entry 9

Symbols

Below each entry you will see some symbols, which are explained at the very back of the book. They are based on information given to us by owners. However, things do change: bikes may be under repair or WiFi may have been added. Please use the symbols as a guide rather than an absolute statement of fact. Owners occasionally bend their own rules, so it is worth asking if you may take your child, for example, even if their entry doesn't have the symbol.

Children – The symbol is given owners who accept children of any age. It does not mean they will necessarily have cots, highchairs, safety equipment etc, so do check. If an owner welcomes children but only those above a certain age, this is stated at the end of the description. Even these folk may accept your younger child if you are the only guests. Many who say no to children do so not because they don't like them but because they may have a steep stair, an unfenced pond or they find balancing the needs of mixed age groups too challenging.

Rooms

We tell you if a bedroom is a double, twin/double (ie with zip and link beds), suite (with a sitting area), or single. Owners can often juggle beds or bedrooms, so do talk to them before you book. Most bedrooms in our B&Bs and hotels have an en suite bath or shower room; we only mention bathroom details when they do not. Please check for full room details for self-catering places.

Meals

In our B&Bs breakfast is included in the room price, unless we say otherwise. Most hotels charge extra for breakfast and we have given the price where this is the case. Some of our hotels offer a half-board option, and some of our B&Bs will arrange an evening meal on request.

Bookings and cancellations

Do be clear about the room booked, the price, and whether it includes any meals. Owners may send you a booking form or contrat de location (tenancy contract) which must be filled in and returned, and commits both sides. Requests for deposits vary; some are non-refundable, and some owners may charge you for the whole of the booked stay in advance. Some cancellation policies are more stringent than others. If owners hold your credit card details they may deduct a cancellation fee from it and not contact you to discuss this. Ask them to explain their cancellation policy clearly before booking.

Payment

Few B&B owners take credit cards; those that do have the appropriate symbol. Most will usually accept euro travellers' cheques; other currency cheques are unpopular because of commission charges. Most hotels will accept MasterCard and Visa. For self-catering places the balance of the rent is normally payable at least eight weeks before the start of the holiday; a few owners take credit cards, otherwise you will need to send a euro cheque, or a sterling cheque if the owner has a British bank account.

Tax de séjour is a small tax that local councils can levy on all visitors; you may find your bill increased by €0.50-€2 per person per day to cover this.

Map 1

17

Hotel
Bed & breakfast
Self-catering

©Maidenhead Cartographic, 2009

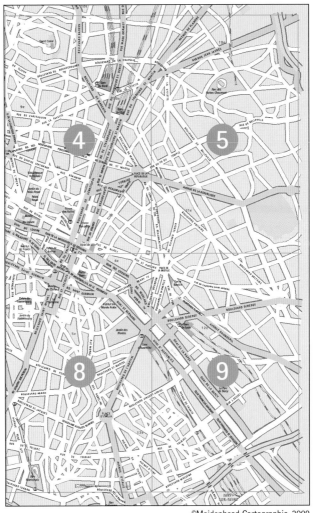

©Maidenhead Cartographic, 2009

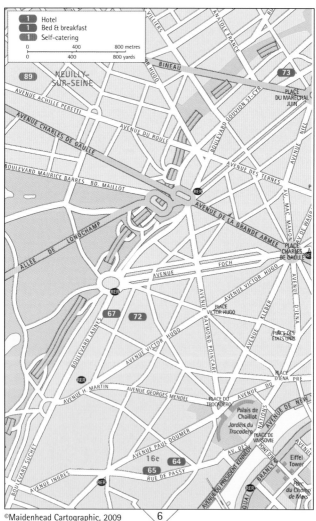

Map 3

21

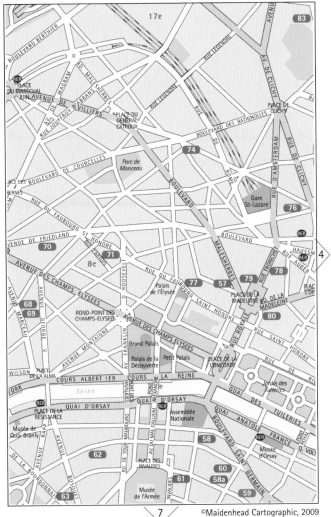

©Maidenhead Cartographic, 2009

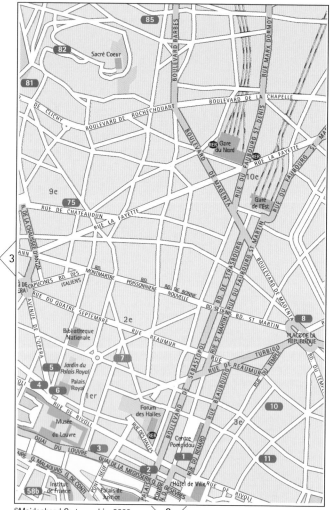

Map 5

23

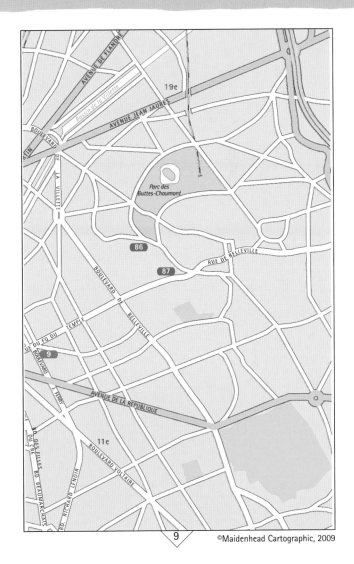

©Maidenhead Cartographic, 2009

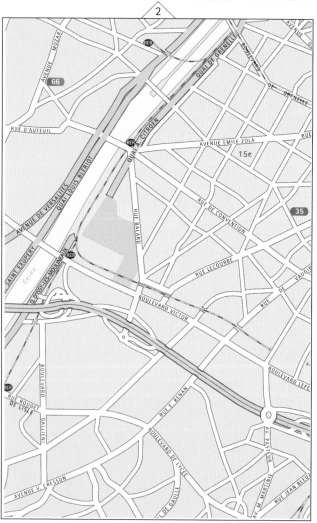

Map 7

25

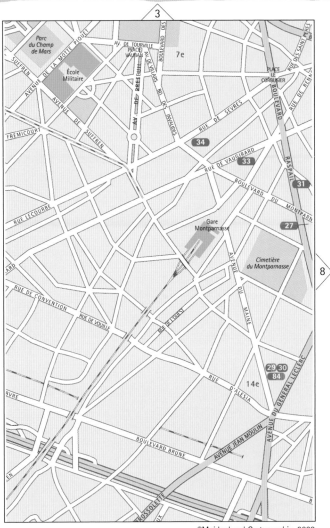

©Maidenhead Cartographic, 2009

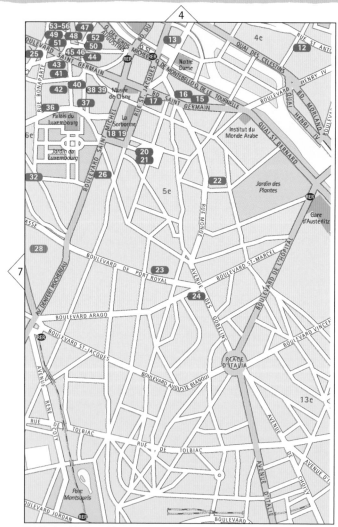

Map 9

27

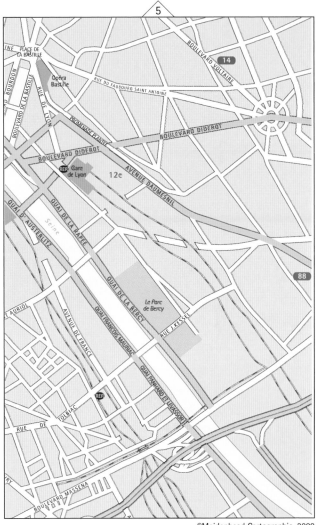

Paris

Hôtel Saint Merry

If you love the old and unusual and don't mind a few stairs, this is for you. The hotel huddles against the late-gothic church of St Merry whose clock tower cornice thrusts its way into the top-floor suite. From brocante and flea market came neo-gothic pieces to make the old house sing and create this astounding environment; in reception you find an elaborate pew, linen-fold panels, a telephone in a confessional. Some rooms are almost majestic, the cheaper ones smaller and more basic, the suite surely Paris's only gothic salon. *Tricky motor access in pedestrian street; no lift in hotel, 4 floors.*

Price	€160–€230. Triples €210–€275. Suite €335–€407.
Rooms	12: 6 doubles, 3 twins, 2 triples, 1 suite for 6.
Meals	Breakfast €11 (served in bedroom only).
Closed	Never.
Directions	Metro: Hôtel de Ville (1, 11), Châtelet (1, 4, 7, 11, 14). RER: Châtelet-Les Halles. Buses: 38, 47, 75. Parking: St Martin.

Pierre Juin
78 rue de la Verrerie, 75004 Paris

Tel	+33 (0)1 42 78 14 15
Web	www.hotelmarais.com

Hôtel Britannique

Hard to imagine such a languid leafy oasis hidden in the historical heart of the city. The hotel is owned by an ex-naval man with a passion for Turner – the great painter's *Jessica* greets you in the lobby, copies of his oils and water colours adorn the laquered grey corridors. Baldaquins discreetly drape over good beds, thick curtains echo the colours in the thin-striped carpets, bathrooms shine. It's lively and fun in the daytime, quietish at night. The semi-basement breakfast room is a honey-warm, rustic country kitchen. It is simply comfortable with no ancient flourishes and friendly staff in stripey waistcoats.

Price	€160-€221. Suite €279-€325.
Rooms	40: 39 twins/doubles, 1 suite.
Meals	Buffet breakfast €13.
Closed	Never.
Directions	Metro: Châtelet.
	RER: Châtelet-Les Halles.

Monsieur J-F Danjou
20 avenue Victoria, 75001 Paris

Tel	+33 (0)1 42 33 74 59
Web	www.hotel-britannique.fr

Entry 2 Map 4

Le Relais du Louvre

The Revolutionaries printed their newsletter in the cellar; the place inspired Puccini's Café Momus in *Bohême* and is utterly delightful, as are the young managers. Antiques and oriental rugs complement the modernity of firm beds and perfect bathrooms. Rooms look either onto the church and along to the Louvre or onto a patio. Suites have exuberant upholstery and heaps of light from mansard windows. The apartment is big and beautiful with fireplace and a superb veranda kitchen. Other, smaller, rooms are luminous and restful. There is a real sense of service, and breakfast comes to you.

Price	€170–€215. Singles €125. Suites €244–€270. Apartment €435. All prices per night.
Rooms	20 + 1: 13 twins/doubles, 5 singles, 2 suites. 1 apartment for 5.
Meals	Breakfast €13 (served in bedroom only, until 2pm). Lunch & dinner on request €10–€30. Wine €7.
Closed	Never.
Directions	Metro: Louvre-Rivoli (1), Pont Neuf (7). RER: Châtelet-Les Halles. Buses: 67, 69, 72, 74, 85.

Sophie Aulnette
19 rue des Prêtres St Germain l'Auxerrois,
75001 Paris

Tel	+33 (0)1 40 41 96 42
Web	www.relaisdulouvre.com

Châtelet district

You will meet a most civilised couple – she bubbly and interested, he quietly studious, a university professor – in their very personal, gently refined apartment where original timbers, saved from the renovator's axe, divide the living room and two friendly cats proclaim the cosiness. It is beautifully done and eminently French, like a warm soft nest, antique-furnished, lots of greenery, interesting art. Mona greatly enjoys her guests and is full of tips on Paris. The attractive, compact guest quarters down the corridor are nicely private with good storage space, pretty quilts and lots of light. *Minimum stay two nights.*

Price	€90.
Rooms	1 twin.
Meals	Restaurants nearby.
Closed	Summer holidays.
Directions	Lift to 3rd floor.
	Metro: Châtelet (1, 4, 7, 11, 14), Pont Neuf (7).
	Parking: Conforama car park, via Rue du Pont Neuf then Rue Boucher.

Mona Pierrot
75001 Paris

Tel   +33 (0)1 42 36 50 65

Hôtel Molière

An enchantingly French hotel. The big lobby/salon is smart and rather grand with its *faux-marbre* columns, potted palms and beige bucket chairs, but the welcome from the desk is gentle and warm. The breakfast room is a delight, red and white striped blinds frame the leafy, cobbled courtyard. There's also a small, deep-chaired salon round the corner for your quiet moments. Bedrooms are just as pretty with judicious use of nostalgic Jouy prints on walls and coordinated checks on quilts. Bathrooms, some vast, some snug, are modern. Interesting paintings and ornaments give the Molière a well-cared-for feel. You will like it here.

Price	€170–€190. Singles €145–€170. Triples €220. Suites €220–€300.
Rooms	32: 14 doubles, 8 twins, 5 singles, 2 triples, 3 suites for 4.
Meals	Breakfast €14.
Closed	Never.
Directions	Metro: Palais Royal-Musée du Louvre (1, 7), Pyramides (7, 14). RER & Roissybus: Auber, Opéra. Buses: 21, 24, 27, 29, 39, 48, 72, 81, 95.

	Patricia & Rémy Perraud
	21 rue Molière, 75001 Paris
Tel	+33 (0)1 42 96 22 01
Web	www.hotel-moliere.fr

Entry 5 Map 4

Hôtel Le Relais Saint Honoré

Unique, the rue Saint Honoré is a delight: once past the gardens of the Presidential Palace it becomes human-sized and unpasteurised, as it meanders along the Tuileries and then charges into an area of higgledy-piggledy streets and iconoclastic shops. The Relais, once a brasserie frequented by Jean Cocteau, dates from 1650. There are 13 small but perfect rooms and two larger suites. You'll sleep on the finest mattresses under the softest blankets enveloped in fine cotton. The beams have been painted to pick up nuances from exquisitely patterned fabrics on curtains and bedheads. Pure comfort with a caring staff.

Price	€206. Suites €305–€345.
Rooms	15: 13 twins/doubles, 2 suites.
Meals	Breakfast €13 (served in bedroom only).
Closed	Never.
Directions	Metro: Tuileries (1), Pyramides (7, 14). RER: Musée d'Orsay. Buses: 68, 72. Parking: Marché Saint Honoré.

Paul Bogaert
308 rue Saint Honoré, 75001 Paris

Tel	+33 (0)1 42 96 06 06
Web	www.relaissainthonore.com

Martinn

A gem of a pied-à-terre, right there in the middle of old Paris. The quiet, neat and secluded cobbled courtyard, hidden behind a huge old heavy wooden coach-entrance door, is your introduction to Martine's ground-floor flat. The door opens straight into the small, uncomplicated and attractive bedroom with its purple tafetta bedcover; beyond are the bathroom and the living room, each beautifully decorated. The whole compact place has every gadget you could require and the corner kitchen is equipped for real cooking. The neighbourhood teems with restaurants, brasseries, cafés, fashionable shops and peaceful semi-pedestrian zones.

Price	€650 per week.
Rooms	1 double; 1 bathroom.
Meals	Restaurants within walking distance.
Closed	Mid-November to mid-February.
Directions	Directions on booking.

Entry 7 Map 4

Martine Jablonski–Cahours
69 rue d'Argout, 75002 Paris
Tel +33 (0)5 62 96 01 07
Web www.mart-inn.com

Garden Saint Martin

In a corner of genuine people's Paris that is attracting trendy cafés, interesting eateries and hip young shoppers, this very modest hotel stands between the tranquil St Martin Canal and the mad dash of the Place de la République. It is one of a row of harmonious, unpretentious 1890s buildings. The new owners have big plans: air conditioning and a refurbished reception. All rooms are gradually being renovated: spring-like décor, primrose-painted furniture, the odd pine-slatted wall and little shower rooms. A super relaxed atmosphere. Don't miss Chez Prune, a lively bar and restaurant on a terrace overlooking the canal.

Price	€60–€100. Singles €72. Triples €108.
Rooms	32: 11 doubles, 10 twins, 6 singles, 5 triples.
Meals	Buffet breakfast €8.
Closed	Never.
Directions	Metro: République (3, 5, 8, 9, 11). RER: Gare du Nord. Buses: 54, 56, 75. Parking: Boulevard Magenta (consult hotel).

Monsieur & Madame Depardieu
35 rue Yves Toudic, 75010 Paris

Tel	+33 (0)1 42 40 17 72
Web	www.hotel-gardensaintmartin-paris.com

L'Appart de la Folie-Méricourt

Pascal and Pascal, who live next door, are the most attentive owners you could hope for and their Paris pad is young at heart and sweetly done. Across the front windows of L'Appart, a fancy wrought-iron balcony where you can watch the world go by. The double bedroom is lime green and pink, the sitting/twin room beyond red-splashed. You will find a well-supplied kitchen with your breakfast basics and homemade jams. You are in a good, authentic part of Paris with shops, cafés, restaurants and entertainment of all sorts. And such nice, friendly neighbours. *Minimum stay two nights.*

Price	€95. Extra person €20. Includes breakfast.
Rooms	1 double, 1 twin/double, sharing bathroom; 2 extra beds available.
Meals	Restaurants nearby.
Closed	Never.
Directions	Metro: Saint Ambroise (9), Oberkampf (5,9) Buses: 56, 96. Parking: République (50 rue de Malte).

Pascal Minault
20 rue de la Folie Méricourt, 75011 Paris

Tel	+33 (0)1 77 15 69 54
Web	www.appartement-hotes-folie-mericourt.com

Bonne Nuit Paris

Absolute Paris, 300 years old but not grand, beams galore and modern comforts, independent rooms and a warm family welcome, little streets, friendly markets: this is real privilege. Charming, intelligent Jean-Luc serves his own honey, Denise's jams and fresh baguette in their generous, rambling living room. Guest rooms are on the floor below. Each has a fun-lovingly colourful shower room, a lot of quirk (the last word in creative basins) and an appealing mix of old woodwork and contemporary prints. Simplicity, panache and personality, real attention and service are the hallmarks: you will feel well cared for.

Price	€150. Extra person €75.
Rooms	3: 2 doubles, 1 triple.
Meals	Restaurants within walking distance.
Closed	Rarely.
Directions	Metro: République (2, 3, 5, 8, 11). Buses: 20, 46, 56, 65, 75. Parking: 3 car parks, €50 for 3 days.

Denise & Jean-Luc Marchand
63 rue Charlot, 75003 Paris

Tel	+33 (0)1 42 71 83 56
Web	www.bonne-nuit-paris.com

Hôtel de la Bretonnerie

The Bretonnerie's 17th-century timber frame embraces a pleasing mix of intimacy and airy gracefulness; the wrought-iron, wooden-railed staircase is an elegant reminder of that Parisian talent for grandeur. Descend to the breakfast room, an atmospheric bare-stone vaulted cellar and ascend to richly-coloured bedrooms off twisty split-level corridors. One large two-windowed corner room has yellow Jouy-style 'brocade' walls, a rich brown carpet, square yellow quilts on pure white, a big marble bathroom. Another fine suite has space to dance, oodles of pink chintz, old furniture. Impeccably smart yet cosy, with utterly delightful staff.

Price	€135–€165. Family rooms €190–€215. Suite €190.
Rooms	29: 22 twins/doubles, 6 family rooms for 3-4, 1 suite.
Meals	Continental-plus breakfast €9.50.
Closed	Never.
Directions	Metro: Hôtel de Ville (1, 11). RER: Châtelet-Les Halles. Buses: 47, 72, 74, 75. Parking: Baudoyer, Lobau.

Philippe Bidal
22 rue Sainte Croix de la Bretonnerie,
75004 Paris

Entry 11 Map 4

| Tel | +33 (0)1 48 87 77 63 |
| Web | www.hotelbretonnerie.com |

Hôtel du 7è Art

The Seventh Art is French for cinema and there is a lively bar where log fires burn in winter and you can buy mementos of the great screen names. Black and white is the theme throughout – viz. that checked floor in the bar/breakfast room – and old film posters decorate the walls. Up the black carpeted stairs, the bedrooms are softly, un-showily decorated – some hessian walls, some pine slatting, brown carpets and piqué bedcovers. Some rooms are small, the largest are on the top floor, the atmosphere is peaceful (the bar closes at midnight), the street is full of antique shops and the oldest part of Paris is all around you.

Price	€90–€145. Single €65.
Rooms	23: 15 doubles, 7 twins, 1 single. Extra beds available.
Meals	Continental-plus breakfast €8.
Closed	Never.
Directions	Metro: St Paul (1), Pont Marie (7), Sully Morland (7). RER: Châtelet-Les Halles. Buses: 69, 96. Parking: Pont Marie, Rue Saint Antoine.

Michel & Yolène
20 rue Saint Paul, 75004 Paris

Tel	+33 (0)1 44 54 85 00
Web	www.paris-hotel-7art.com

Entry 12 Map 8

Hôtel du Jeu de Paume

The Île Saint Louis is the most exclusive 17th-century village in Paris and this renovated 'tennis court' – three storeys soar to the timbers – is an exceptional sight. Add genuine care from mother-and-daughter owners, fresh flowers and super staff. Smallish rooms give onto quiet courtyards, have rich fabrics, old beams, parquet. Some rooms have tiny staircases, some have little terraces; the apartments over the street have tall windows, space and style. We love it for its sense of history, feel of home and unconventional attitudes. The lounge has chocolate brown sofas round a carved fireplace, and Scoop the soft gold dog. *Let Mme Prache know if your stay spans an anniversary.*

Price	€285–€360. Singles €185–€255. Apartments €600–€900. All prices per night.
Rooms	30 + 2: 20 twins/doubles, 7 singles, 3 suites. 2 apartments for 4–6.
Meals	Breakfast €18.
Closed	Rarely.
Directions	Metro: Pont Marie (7), Cité (4), St Paul (1). RER: St Michel-Notre Dame. Bus: 67. Parking: Pont Marie.

Entry 13 Map 8

	Elyane Prache & Nathalie Heckel 54 rue St Louis en l'Ile, 75004 Paris
Tel	+33 (0)1 43 26 14 18
Web	www.jeudepaumehotel.com

B&B Guénot

A garden! In central Paris! A restful corner and quiet, well-travelled hosts with their 10-year-old son to greet you after a day of cultural excitements. The architect-renovated apartment, a delight of clever design, embraces their private garden. All rooms turn towards the greenery, including your charming compact bedroom with its timber floor, large oil painting and wonderful bathroom so, once through the door that leads off the red-leather sitting room, you are in this intimate space, there to enjoy your wide window onto bird-twitter. A generous continental breakfast – and you're ready for more museum fare. *Minimum stay two nights.*

Price	€90–€100.
Rooms	1 double.
Meals	Restaurants within walking distance.
Closed	Rarely.
Directions	Metro: Nation (1, 2, 6, 9), Rue des Boulets (9). Buses: 26, 56, 57, 86. RER: Nation.

Anne–Lise Valadon
4 passage Guénot, 75011 Paris

Tel	+33 (0)1 42 74 23 84
Web	www.bb-guenot.com

Hôtel Abbatial Saint Germain

Michel Sahuc is relaxed and affable and his style informs his hotel: the receptionist may choose the music playing over the desk but the salon with its long, caramel-coloured leather sofas is quiet. Rooms are mostly a decent size, some special ones are on a corner, and almost all have two windows; some bathrooms have sliding doors and rain-head showers. A few rooms at the top have fabulous views swinging round from the colonnade of the Panthéon to the north rose of Notre Dame on her island. The lush foliage on the trees fronting the hotel and a scattering of small neighborhood bistros are a plus. A friendly, unpretentious place.

Price	€160-€195. Singles €140. Triples €220.
Rooms	43: 22 doubles, 13 twins, 5 singles, 3 triples.
Meals	Continental buffet breakfast €12.
Closed	Never.
Directions	Metro: Maubert Mutualité (10).
	RER: St Michel-Notre Dame.
	Buses: 47, 63, 86, 87.
	Parking: St Germain.

	Michel Sahuc
	46 boulevard St Germain, 75005 Paris
Tel	+33 (0)1 46 34 02 12
Web	www.abbatial.com

Entry 15 Map 8

Hôtel Agora Saint Germain

Deep in the heart of the Latin Quarter, one of the oldest centres of learning in Europe, here is a quiet place to stay. The generous well-lit hall, the pretty glassed-in planted patio and the comfortable armchairs are greeting enough – then you'll be welcomed by the charming receptionist, or by Madame Sahuc herself, youthful and bright. There is an atmosphere of relaxed, feminine attention to detail here including the black and white photgraphs which give it a modern feel. Bedrooms have been recently renovated in sober colours, good fabrics and sparkling chrome-trimmed bathrooms. A good reliable address and a lively market next door.

Price	€189–€195. Singles €149. Family room €210.
Rooms	39: 2 doubles, 9 twins, 27 singles, 1 family room for 3.
Meals	Continental buffet breakfast €11.
Closed	Never.
Directions	Metro: Maubert Mutualité (10). RER: St Michel–Notre Dame. Buses: 47, 63, 86, 87, 24. Parking: St Germain.

Pascale Sahuc
42 rue des Bernardins, 75005 Paris

Tel	+33 (0)1 46 34 13 00
Web	www.agorasaintgermain.com

Hôtel du Collège de France

An atmosphere of solid, well-established family comfort: exposed stones, lots of wood, soft armchairs, good lighting. The breakfast room is warmly red, with old Parisian prints and a Madonna. Bedrooms are mostly not large, but each has a full-length mirror and a thoroughly practical desk unit. The décor is quite colourful in places with coordinated botanical fabrics, and soft quilts – it is careful and restful, beds are new and bathrooms are fine. Rooms at the top are worth the walk up from the fifth floor. Above all, a genuinely friendly reception is assured, as are generous breakfasts and good value on a quiet street. *Don't miss bistro Le Pré Verre across the street.*

Price	€90–€145.
Rooms	29: 23 doubles, 6 twins.
Meals	Buffet breakfast €10.
Closed	Never.
Directions	Metro: St Michel (4), Maubert-Mutualité (10). RER: St Michel-Notre Dame. Buses: 21, 24, 27, 38, 63, 85, 86, 87. Parking: Maubert-Mutualité.

		Jean Marc
		7 rue Thénard, 75005 Paris
	Tel	+33 (0)1 43 26 78 36
Entry 17 Map 8	Web	www.hotel-collegedefrance.com

Hôtel des 3 Collèges

Two breakfasts are available: a quick bite for those on the run or a more elaborate repast for those who want a slow start and enjoy watching busy people rush past big windows. The walls are hung with ancient maps showing the Latin Quarter through the ages: the building's foundations were probably laid when Lutetia was capital of Roman Gaul. In a corner, the 22-metre well still holds water. Bedrooms are simple, with white furniture and pastel-hued bedcovers; good functional bathrooms have Roger & Gallet toiletries plus a clothes line. A very pleasant and reasonable place to stay and Jonathan will give you an excellent bus map.

Price	€102–€150. Singles €82. Triples €150–€170.
Rooms	44: 27 doubles, 5 twins, 10 singles, 2 triples.
Meals	Breakfast €4.20-€8.
Closed	Never.
Directions	Metro: Cluny La Sorbonne (10), St Michel (4). RER: Luxembourg, St Michel-Notre Dame. Buses: 21, 27, 38, 63, 82, 84, 86, 87. Parking: Rue Soufflot.

Jonathan Wyplosz
16 rue Cujas, 75005 Paris

Tel	+33 (0)1 43 54 67 30
Web	www.3colleges.com

Hôtel de la Sorbonne

Pascale & Corinne Moncelli, who own a selection of the most interesting hotels on the Left Bank, have worked their magic again with this little hotel just across from the Sorbonne. They brought daylight into the tiny lobby with a glass and metal structure and it now glows in a halo of turquoise fabric. The breakfast room is similarly bright and will jolt you into wakefulness even before coffee is served. Rooms are small, but splendid wallpaper, thick carpeting, real showers and the fresh decor bring a sense of well-being. The ultra-modern touch is an iMac in every room with free access to email or your favourite film.

Price	€70–€350.
Rooms	38 doubles.
Meals	Breakfast €12 (€15 in bedroom).
Closed	Never.
Directions	Metro: Cluny-Sorbonne. RER: Luxembourg. Buses: 21, 27, 38, 63, 82, 84, 86, 97. Parking: Rue Soufflot.

David Germain
6 rue Victor Cousin, 75005 Paris

Tel	+33 (0)1 43 59 58 08
Web	www.hotelsorbonne.com

Hôtel du Panthéon

Sainte Geneviève saved the Parisians from Attila in 451 and was declared their patron saint. This is her neighbourhood: her abbey is now a prestigious lycée; a tiny squiggle of a street and wonderful library opposite the hotel bear her name. The hotel has the feel of an 18th-century townhouse: the rooms are Louis XV 'country style' with beams and exquisite fabric on the walls; the beds, some four-postered and canopied, are kept white, their bedheads and coverlets in another pattern. Curtains frame views onto the majestic Panthéon in the centre of the square. Bathrooms are luxurious – one is bigger than the room – and the welcome perfect.

Price	€99–€310. Family rooms €184–€470.
Rooms	36: 34 twins/doubles, 2 family rooms for 2-3.
Meals	Breakfast €13.
Closed	Never.
Directions	Metro: Cardinal Lemoine (10). RER: Luxembourg, St Michel-Notre Dame. Buses: 21, 27, 38, 58, 82, 84, 85, 89. Parking: Rue Soufflot.

Mathieu Paygamban
19 Place du Panthéon, 75005 Paris
Tel   +33 (0)1 43 54 32 95
Web   www.hoteldupantheon.com

Hôtel des Grands Hommes

You reach the hotel by crossing the expanse of the round neo-classical Place du Panthéon; then the doors of the hotel slide open and you slip into a knock-out Empire style. Urns, columns and classical curlicues set the tone, while in an intimate alcove the plush of velvet settees and aubergine-striped curtains invite discreet conversations. The great dome has a surreal proximity to the hotel from the ground floor to the top-floor rooms with their big terraces, some with views to the Sacré Cœur. Rooms are jewel boxes of canopied beds, Pompeii-like frescoes, exquisite chandeliers, toile de Jouy. It's all pure magic.

Price	€108–€310. Suites €215–€430. Family rooms €184–€282.
Rooms	31: 23 twins/doubles, 5 family rooms for 3, 3 suites.
Meals	Breakfast €13.
Closed	Never.
Directions	Metro: Cardinal Lemoine (10). RER: Luxembourg, St Michel-Notre Dame. Buses: 21, 27, 38, 58, 82, 84, 85, 89. Parking: Rue Soufflot.

	Madame Hery
	17 place du Panthéon, 75005 Paris
Tel	+33 (0)1 46 34 19 60
Web	www.hoteldesgrandshommes.com

Entry 21 Map 8

Notre Dame district

At the end of the street are the Seine and the glory of Notre Dame. In a grand old building, up a 17th-century staircase, the unaffected tall-windowed rooms look down to peace in a little garden. The low-mezzanined family room has a bathroom off the internal landing where a simple breakfast is laid beside the spiral stair. Upstairs, the second, smaller, room has the bed in the corner and a fresh décor. Madame is polyglot, active and eager to help when she is available, and leaves breakfast ready if she has to go out. She and her daughter appreciate the variety of contact guests bring.

Price	€85–€150.
Rooms	2: 1 double, 1 quadruple with separate bathroom.
Meals	Continental breakfast left ready if owner has to go out.
Closed	Rarely.
Directions	From street, enter 2407. In courtyard, ring house bell on left.
	Metro: Maubert-Mutualité (10).
	RER: St Michel.
	Parking: Book ahead.

Brigitte Chatignoux
75005 Paris

Tel   +33 (0)1 43 25 27 20

Entry 22 Map 8

The Five Hotel

The rooms are small, sensual and playful – reserve your choice of scent when booking. White covers on the best mattresses, a ribbon of colour draped across each; splashes of turquoise on a wall or a cornflower-blue pattern on a sliding panel over a window. The low-key lacquered original art work is the inspiration, an integral part of the décor, not just an add-on. Fine fibre-optic lights shower down from ceilings and shine like tiny diamonds in bathroom tiles. A canopied bed in one room, a floating mattress in another and a suite with a jacuzzi on a terrace.

Price	€180-€320. Singles €150-€180. Suite €320-€420.
Rooms	19: 8 doubles, 5 twins, 5 singles, 1 suite for 1-4.
Meals	Breakfast €15. Lunch & dinner €20.
Closed	Never.
Directions	Metro: Les Gobelins, Censier Daubenton (7). RER: Port Royal. Buses: 21, 91. Parking: Marché des Patriaches.

Monsieur Philippe Vaurs
3 rue Flatters, 75005 Paris

Tel	+33 (0)1 43 31 74 21
Web	www.thefivehotel.com

Hôtel Résidence Les Gobelins

Street, hotel, owners are all quiet, attentive and unassuming. Workers in the great Gobelins tapestry shops lived in this area and it was never smart, but nearby is the entertaining, bohemian Rue Mouffetard – eating houses, mosque, lively market and left-wing culture. The lounge, with cushioned wicker furniture, and the breakfast room lie round the honeysuckle-hung courtyard. Bedrooms and bathrooms are simple restful and harmonious. White bedspreads sparkle and the green and dark red rattan furniture is ageing with grace. The Poiriers' gentle unobtrusive friendliness reminds us that the family used to keep a *pension de famille*.

Price	€89–€95.
Rooms	32 doubles.
Meals	Breakfast €8.50. Restaurant 100m.
Closed	Never.
Directions	Metro: Gobelins (7).
	RER: Port Royal.
	Buses: 27, 47, 83, 91.
	Parking: Place d'Italie.

Jennifer & Philippe Poirier
9 rue des Gobelins, 75013 Paris

Tel   +33 (0)1 47 07 26 90

Les Toits de Paris

The attic-level flat, the guest room opposite and their most courteously welcoming young owners (with baby Marius) are all of a lovely piece: modest, quiet, clothed in gentle earthy colours, natural materials and discreet manners. You will feel instantly at ease in this cultured atmosphere. Across the landing, your quiet and intimate room has a super-comfy bed, a convertible sofa and a darling little writing desk beneath the sloping beams while the beautiful bathroom has everything. Walk round 'the village', discover its quirky little shops, its restaurants for all tastes and budgets – then head for the riches of central Paris. *No lift, 3rd floor.*

Price	€120.
Rooms	1 double with single sofabed.
Meals	Restaurants nearby.
Closed	Rarely.
Directions	Metro: Commerce (8), Émile Zola (10), Convention (12). RER: Javel. Buses: 62, 70, 80, 88.

Matthieu & Sophie de Montenay
25 rue de l'Abbé Groult, 75015 Paris
Tel   +33 (0)6 60 57 92 05
Web   www.chambrehotesparis.fr

Entry 25 Map 8

Hôtel Les Jardins du Luxembourg

Freud once tramped this cul-de-sac when he stayed here in the winter of 1885-86. The original beams are still on view in some rooms, especially those under the eaves. We can imagine Freud sitting in front of the fireplace in the little salon; Art Deco chairs and good lighting give it an intimate feel. The reception area, by contrast, is a big open space, and room keys hang over a handsome mahogany desk that doubles as a bar. Keep your eye out for the patterned tiles here: a delightful ochre and orange checkerboard in the breakfast room and trompe-l'oeil lizards and vines in the bathrooms, some of which have four-legged bath tubs.

Price	€135-€170. Singles €143.
Rooms	26: 18 doubles, 7 twins, 1 single.
Meals	Breakfast €11.
Closed	Never.
Directions	Metro: Cluny la Sorbonne (10). RER: Luxembourg. Buses: 21, 27, 38, 82, 84, 85, 89. Parking: Private parking available.

Hélène Touber
5 Impasse Royer Collard, 75005 Paris

Tel	+33 (0)1 40 46 08 88
Web	www.les-jardins-du-luxembourg.com

Entry 26 Map 8

Hôtel Raspail Montparnasse

Below the satisfyingly genuine 1924 frontage, the old doors spring towards you as you approach – 20th-century magic. There's old-style generosity in the high Art Deco lobby with its ceiling fans, leather chairs and play of squares and curves, and the intimate hide-away bar with its leopard skin stools is a reminder of all-night conversations about art and love. In the bedrooms gauze curtains, elegant sidetables, wooden bedboards and desks. To each floor a colour: quiet grey, sunny ochre, powder-puff blue; to each landing a stained-glass window. Some rooms have the added perk of an Eiffel Tower view; below, Montparnasse bustles crazily.

Price	€129-€220. Suites €225-€280.
Rooms	38: 36 twins/doubles, 2 suites.
Meals	Breakfast €10.
Closed	Never.
Directions	Metro: Vavin (4), Raspail (4, 6). RER: Port Royal. Buses: 58, 68, 82, 91. Parking: Boulevard du Montparnasse.

Madame Christiane Martinent
203 boulevard Raspail, 75014 Paris
Tel   +33 (0)1 43 20 62 86

8 rue Campagne Première

Behind Montparnasse, in a cobbled alley, you will find what looks like a garden shed. Enter: the shed turns into a smart hall, beyond it an indoor 'garden', double-height and full of happy plants and light, and generous space for two. It is the nicest, most unexpected hideaway imaginable; highly original and delighting in a tiny, pretty kitchen. Up a steep staircase, the bedroom, with three cottage windows, looks into the living room. There's a study with a big glass writing table and single divan, a laundry room and a splendid black and white bathroom that gives onto a courtyard straight from a provincial backwater.

Price	€1,000 per week; €3,000 per month.
Rooms	1 double, 1 sofabed; 1 bathroom, 1 separate wc.
Meals	Restaurant 20m.
Closed	Never.
Directions	Directions on booking.

Alice de Chambure
75014 Paris
Tel   +33 (0)3 86 76 10 10

Montparnasse district

A little house in a quiet alley behind Montparnasse? It's not a dream and Janine, a live-wire cinema journalist who has lived in Canada, welcomes B&B guests to her pretty wood-ceilinged kitchen/diner; she's a night bird so DIY breakfast will be laid for you. The square bedroom across the book-lined hall, a pleasing mix of warm fabrics, honeycomb tiles, old chest and contemporary art, has a good new pine bathroom. In summer rent the whole flat, its richly French sitting room with art, antiques and music, its adorable central patio, superbly rich second bedroom and bathroom. *Minimum stay two nights.*

Price	€70. Singles €60. Self-catering €950–€1,000 per week.
Rooms	1 + 1: 1 double & bathroom.
	Self-catering: 2 doubles, 2 bathrooms.
Meals	Restaurants nearby.
Closed	B&B October–June. Self-catering July–September.
Directions	Metro: Gaîté (13).
	RER: Denfert-Rochereau.
	Buses: 28, 58.

Janine Euvrard
75014 Paris

Tel   +33 (0)1 43 27 19 43

Montparnasse district

Filled with books, paintings and objects from around the world, the Monbrisons' intimate little flat is old and fascinating. Lively American Cynthia, an art-lover, and quintessentially French Christian, knowledgeable about history, wine and cattle-breeding, offer great hospitality, thoughtful conversation, and may take you to historical landmarks. Their guest room, quiet and snug, has a king-size bed and a good bathroom with views of trees. Twice a week, the open market brings the real food of France to your street; shops, cafés and restaurants abound; you can walk to the Luxembourg Gardens.

Price	€85.
Rooms	1 twin/double.
Meals	Occasional dinner with wine, €20.
Closed	August.
Directions	Metro: Edgar Quinet (6), Montparnasse (4, 6, 12, 13).

Christian & Cynthia de Monbrison
75014 Paris
Tel   +33 (0)1 43 35 20 87

Le Sainte Beuve

This beautifully decorated hotel exudes an atmosphere of designer luxury. The extraordinarily attractive salon has superb silk curtains, an old marble fireplace, modern paintings and old prints. It is all small and intimate with attentive, efficient staff. Bedrooms come in ancient and modern finery with at least one antique per room – a leather-topped desk, a walnut dressing-table, an armoire, and 18th/19th-century pictures. The *Sainte Beuve* room is dazzling. Bathrooms are superbly modern with bathrobes and fine toiletries. Breakfast comes from the famous Mulot bakery and you can run it off in the Luxembourg Gardens.

Price	€155–€365. Suite €315–€365.
Rooms	22: 5 doubles, 16 twins, 1 suite for 2.
Meals	Breakfast €15.
Closed	Rarely.
Directions	Metro: Notre Dame des Champs (12), Vavin (4). RER: Port-Royal. Parking: Montparnasse.

Entry 31 Map 7

Monsieur Ferrero
9 rue Sainte-Beuve, 75006 Paris
Tel   +33 (0)1 45 48 20 07
Web   www.paris-hotel-charme.com

Pension Les Marronniers

It's an honest-to-goodness *pension de famille*, one of the last, so if you're young and penniless or old and nostalgic, head for Marie's home overlooking the Luxembourg Gardens – it's been in her family since the 1930s. There are portraits and photographs; statues and plants; a carved, green armoire topped with a motley crew of candlesticks. Marie, down-to-earth and compassionate, coddles her guests and loves cooking for them. The bedrooms for short-stayers have less personality than the dining and drawing room and most share washing facilities. What counts is the welcome, the tradition and the food. *No lift, 1st floor.*

Price	Half-board €40–€67 p.p. Weekly & monthly rentals.
Rooms	12 twins/doubles (6 with shower, 6 sharing bathrooms).
Meals	Half-board only, except Saturdays & Sundays (brunch on Saturdays).
Closed	Never.
Directions	Metro: Vavin (4), Notre Dame des Champs (12). RER: Luxembourg. Buses: 58, 82, 83. Parking: Rue Auguste Comte.

Marie Poirier
78 rue d'Assas, 75006 Paris

Tel	+33 (0)1 43 26 37 71
Web	www.pension-marronniers.com

Trianon Rive Gauche

On the Rive Gauche, three steps from the Sorbonne, three minutes from the Jardins de Luxembourg. A pair of buildings run up eight storeys linked by a staircase that wraps its graceful self around the cage lift… and the rooms at the top get the views: gaze over Parisian rooftops to the Eiffel Tower and the Sacré Cœur. Step into a black, white and silver reception manned by delightful staff and then on to comfortable bedrooms, not huge – save for the largest – but a fair size for Paris. There are fabric-covered walls in dark orange and mustard, brown quilted bedspreads and heavy drapes. Bathrooms, though tiny, are sparklier.

Price	€109-€198. Singles €101-€165. Triples €165-€245. Quadruples €250-€270.
Rooms	110: 60 doubles, 34 twins, 5 singles, 9 triples, 2 quadruples.
Meals	Buffet breakfast €14 (continental breakfast included).
Closed	Never.
Directions	Metro: Cluny, Odéon (10), St Michel (4). RER: Luxembourg (B). Buses: 21, 27, 38, 82. Parking: Rue de l'Ecole de Médecine or rue Soufflot.

Madame Perrine Henneveux
1bis & 3 rue de Vaugirard, 75006 Paris

Tel +33 (0)1 43 29 88 10
Web www.hoteltrianonrivegauche.com

Hôtel Mayet

Youthful and fun. In the oak-floored lobby, the reception desk is an office unit lookalike with two black meeting-room lamps overhead. To left and right, artists have been at bright, drippy mural work, there are deep sofas and venetian blinds. Here reigns smiling Hélène: she's been with Laurence for years. Walk down to breakfast: every step is carpeted a different, vibrant colour; the stone vault houses self-service shelves and two vending machines. Bedrooms are in grey, white and dark red, with 'office' furniture, good little bathrooms and excellent bedding. A quiet street in a great neighbourhood and, as we said, huge fun.

Price	€120–€140.
Rooms	23 twins/doubles.
Meals	Self-service breakfast included.
Closed	August & Christmas.
Directions	Metro: Duroc (10, 13), Vaneau (10). RER: Invalides, St Michel-Notre Dame. Buses: 28, 39, 70, 82, 87, 89, 92. Parking: Bon Marché.

Laurence Raymond & Hélène Jacquet
3 rue Mayet, 75006 Paris
Tel   +33 (0)1 47 83 21 35
Web   www.mayet.com

Le Madison

Discreet behind a row of trees opposite the vastly celebrated Deux Magots café, the fine Art Deco façade is as supremely Parisian as its antique-filled salons. The enlightened owner has created an artistic and very stylish city hotel: bathrooms have stunning Italian tiling, luminous glass crescents clasp drapes, lift doors carry wonderful artists' impressions of the great names of St Germain. Staff have just the right mix of polite class and friendly cheerfulness and all rooms burst with personality: in a big blue and beige room, a red marble bathroom; in the top-floor suite a triumph of space and light with wraparound views.

Price	€235–€395. Singles €175–€195. Suites €415–€435.
Rooms	52: 46 twins/doubles, 3 singles, 3 suites.
Meals	Breakfast included.
Closed	Never.
Directions	Metro: St Germain des Prés. RER: Saint Michel.

Caroline Demon
143 boulevard Saint Germain, 75006 Paris

Tel	+33 (0)1 40 51 60 00
Web	www.hotel-madison.com

Hôtel Le Clos Médicis

An air of contemporary class here and the attractive countersunk salon has a fire, deep brown armchairs, jungle pictures and a fine stone pillar; beyond it are the Tuscan patio and the delightful young team at reception. A *clos* is a vineyard, and each room is named after a wine. Bedrooms have been redesigned by fashionable names in strong colours and have real fabrics, deep-framed mirrors and sophisticated wildlife prints. One room has a terrace, another is a cleverly-arranged duplex; all are said to be soundproofed and, if not always very big, are most comfortable. Add that lively sense of hospitality, and it's excellent.

Price	€180–€270. Singles from €150. Family room & duplex €310–€435.
Rooms	38: 16 doubles, 20 twins/doubles, 1 family room for 3, 1 duplex.
Meals	Buffet breakfast €13.
Closed	Never.
Directions	Metro: Odéon (4,10). RER: Luxembourg. Buses: 21, 38, 82, 84, 85, 89. Parking: Rue Soufflot.

Olivier Méallet
56 rue Monsieur le Prince, 75006 Paris

Tel	+33 (0)1 43 29 10 80
Web	www.hotelclosmedicisparis.com

Entry 36 Map 8

Hôtel Michelet Odéon

A budget find in an extraordinary setting right next door to the beautiful 18th-century L'Odéon. The breakfast room off the day-lit lobby sets the tone: big padded cushions line a wall in chocolate brown, taupe and redcurrant; it's simple and sober with a warm mix of colour and materials. Upstairs Delphine skilfully uses earth tones with a zebra-patterned rug, silky taffeta curtains and thick bedspreads. Modern bathrooms are sparkling-tiled in white with a discreet mosaic trim. From some rooms you can see the theatre, from others the Luxembourg Gardens. It's basic, in good taste and in a prime position for Left Bank roaming.

Price	€122.50–€132.50. Single €100. Family rooms €175–€195. Suites €220.
Rooms	42: 35 twins/doubles, 1 single, 3 family rooms for 3, 1 family room for 4, 2 suites for 4.
Meals	Breakfast €14.
Closed	Never.
Directions	Metro: Odéon (4,10). RER: Luxembourg. Buses: 21, 27, 38, 58, 84, 85, 89, 63, 87. Parking: Marché St Germain des Prés.

Delphine Mouton
6 Place de l'Odéon, 75006 Paris

Tel	+33 (0)1 53 10 05 60
Web	www.hotelmicheletodeon.com

Hôtel Jardin de l'Odéon

When the cubists 'discovered' African art, revered were most things ethnic. Hence the marriage of tall ebony Egyptian scribes, an Ashanti statue and the reclining nude à la Picasso overlooking the Art Deco salon. Just beyond the pleasant, airy lounge and breakfast area, the sound of a fountain emerges from a jasmine-planted terrace. Renovations are recent: curtains and bedcovers mix and match handsome fabric; rooms at the back have garden views, others have exquisite private terraces. Sylvia will see to it that you are well taken care of. All this on a quiet, tiny street leading down to St Germain or up to the Jardins de Luxembourg.

Price	€70–€370. Family rooms €166–€450.
Rooms	41: 19 doubles, 17 twins, 1 single, 4 family rooms.
Meals	Breakfast €13.
Closed	Never.
Directions	Metro: Odéon (4,10), Luxembourg. RER: St Michel-Notre Dame. Buses: 21, 27, 38, 58, 63, 82, 84, 85, 86, 87, 89. Parking: École de Médecine.

Sylvia Harrault
7 rue Casimir Delavigne, 75006 Paris
Tel   +33 (0)1 53 10 28 50
Web   www.hoteljardinodeonparis.com

Grand Hôtel des Balcons

Remarkable value, super people and a daily feast of a breakfast (sumptuous cooked spread, fresh fruit salad...) that's free on your birthday! Having decorated her Art Nouveau hotel by taking inspiration from the floral 1890s staircase windows, Denise now teaches *ikebana* and flowers the house – brilliantly – while her son Jean-François and his wife manage – charmingly. Rooms are simple and at the back you may be woken by the birds. The five big family rooms have smart décor, parquet floors, good bathrooms; other rooms are not big but purpose-made table units use the space judiciously and front rooms have balconies with window boxes.

Price	€110–€175. Singles €85–€175. Family rooms €220.
Rooms	50: 25 doubles, 14 twins, 6 singles, 5 family rooms for 4.
Meals	Breakfast €12.
Closed	Never.
Directions	Metro: Odéon (4, 10). RER: Luxembourg. Buses: 21, 27, 24, 58, 63, 86, 87, 95, 96. Parking: École de Médecine.

Jean-François André
3 rue Casimir Delavigne, 75006 Paris

Tel	+33 (0)1 46 34 78 50
Web	www.balcons.com

Hôtel Louis II

Imagination has triumphed in this 18th-century house and even the smallest rooms (some are very snug) have huge personality. Two have dazzling wraparound trompe-l'œil pictures set into the timber frame, one has an antique door as a bedhead, all have beams. On the top floor, you sleep under sloping rafters in a long room with sculpted gold sconces beside each bed. Descend to a refined breakfast in the golden elegance of the big salon with its magnificent fanning beams and superb double-sided curtains. Gilt-framed mirrors, a ship's figurehead, fine antique tables, and Turkey rugs on old terracotta tiles complete the picture.

Price	€195–€220. Triples €310.
Rooms	22: 20 twins/doubles, 2 triples.
Meals	Breakfast €15.
Closed	Never.
Directions	Metro: Odéon. RER: St Michel-Notre Dame.

	Guillaume Jouvin 2 rue Saint Sulpice, 75006 Paris
Tel	+33 (0)1 46 33 13 80
Web	www.hotel-louis2.com

Hôtel Odéon Saint-Germain

Once across the threshold of this small hotel you will be swept away by the feeling of understated luxury. There is an honesty bar in the lobby along with black-and-white striped armchairs and a comfy toffee-coloured sofa facing an ancient stone fireplace. Some high-ceilinged rooms have silk canopies, others have chaise longues for lounging, or a luscious panel of flower-patterned raw silk behind the leather headboards. Sounds are muffled – even the doors to the rooms have been padded for everyone's comfort. Breakfast is a feast of homemade fruit compotes and cakes, prunes plumped in a cinnamon syrup and the best pastries that Paris can offer.

Price	€145–€370.
Rooms	27: 15 doubles, 6 twins, 2 singles, 4 triples.
Meals	Breakfast €14.
Closed	Never.
Directions	Metro: Odéon.
	RER: St Michel-Notre Dame.

Monsieur & Madame Triadou
13 rue Saint Sulpice, 75006 Paris
Tel   +33 (0)1 43 25 70 11
Web   www.hotelosg.com

Hôtel Relais Saint Sulpice

On the back doorstep of Saint Sulpice church, this is the perfect hideaway for *Da Vinci Code* fans, or for spotting the literati of Saint Germain des Prés. You might miss the entrance; it's more an entryway into an aristocratic 18th-century home than a door to a hotel. The womb-like salon has mahogany bookcases, backlit objets lining the top shelves, a pair of 1940s armchairs and a big gilt mirror. No reception desk, just a friendly spirit behind a small table to hand out keys to your small but cosy room. A huge glass roof and a bounty of greenery give a winter garden feel to the breakfast room. An exceptional address.

Price	€178–€270. €245 for 3.
Rooms	26: 19 doubles, 7 twins. Extra bed available.
Meals	Breakfast €12.
Closed	Never.
Directions	Metro: Odeon (4, 10), Mabillon (10).
	RER: St Michel-Notre Dame, Luxembourg.
	Buses: 58, 70, 63, 86, 87, 96, 84.
	Parking: Place Saint Sulpice & Marché Saint-Germain.

Hélène Touber
3 rue Garancière, 75006 Paris
Tel   +33 (0)1 46 33 99 00
Web   www.relais-saint-sulpice.com

Entry 42 Map 8

Hôtel le Clément

This delightful little hotel has been in the same family for 100 years and Madame Charrade is the gentlest professional hotelier you could meet. The lobby is cosy and inviting with fireplace, gleaming panelling and bookshelves. From the higher floors, the view across the St Germain marketplace to the towers of St Sulpice church is super; the rooms here have loads of character with their sloping ceilings, if somewhat less space. Back rooms have no view, of course, but peace is guaranteed. Madame's decorative style is southern cottage: small floral prints with good colour combinations; bathrooms are often colourfully tiled.

Price	€123–€144. Triples & family rooms €160.
Rooms	28: 12 doubles, 6 twins, 5 triples, 5 family rooms for 3.
Meals	Buffet breakfast €11.
Closed	Never.
Directions	Metro: St Germain des Prés (4), Mabillon (10). RER: Luxembourg. Buses: 63, 70, 85, 86, 95, 96. Parking: Opposite hotel.

Monsieur & Madame Charrade
6 rue Clément, 75006 Paris

Tel   +33 (0)1 43 26 53 60
Web   www.hotel-clement.fr

Grand Hôtel de l'Univers

You are in an old part of town and the 15th-century effigy of a man leaning on his truncheon, found above the door, remains a mystery. The big airy salon is a surprise with the theatricality of its 18th-century sofa, armchairs and antique dresser set against a huge wall of honey-coloured stone; the bar is a much cosier affair. Rooms are delightful, quiet, and decorated with flair; bathrooms are in marble and chrome. If size is important, opt for the superior or deluxe rooms, they are worth the extra charge. Breakfast in the stone-vaulted cellar is a real treat, with eggs, sausages and fresh orange juice.

Price	€150–€280. Singles €130–€185.
Rooms	33 twins/doubles.
Meals	Buffet breakfast €10.
Closed	Never.
Directions	Metro: Odéon (4,10).
	RER: St Michel-Notre Dame.
	Buses: 58, 63, 70, 86, 96.
	Parking: Rue Mazarine, St Germain des Prés.

Eric Desfaudais
6 rue Grégoire de Tours, 75006 Paris
Tel   +33 (0)1 43 29 37 00
Web   www.hotel-paris-univers.com

Hôtel Prince de Condé

In one of the smallest hotels in the city on one of the most sauntering streets – named after the great river to which it leads – enormous attention to detail. Paris is full of vaulted cellars transformed into breakfast rooms but it is rare to find one done in such style: a red patterned carpet warms the exposed stone and armchairs are clothed in broad stripes and fun patterns. Bedrooms have canopies over beds, cloth-lined walls, an English chair or Napoleon III desk. The large suite gets a jacuzzi tub and swish Italian faucets. Galleries for gazing and people for watching on rue de Seine and the rue Buci nearby.

Price	€150–€300.
Rooms	11: 10 twins/doubles, 1 suite for 2.
Meals	Breakfast €13.
Closed	Never.
Directions	Metro: St Germain des Prés (4), Odéon (4,10), Pont Neuf (7), Mabillon (10). RER: St Michel-Notre Dame. Buses: 58, 70. Parking: Rue Mazarine.

Hélène Touber
39 rue de Seine, 75006 Paris

Tel	+33 (0)1 43 26 71 56
Web	www.prince-de-conde.com

Entry 45 Map 8

Welcome Hôtel

The Welcome sits on one of the trendiest crossroads of Paris where the delightfully twisty, fashionable shopping streets and the legendary cafés of St Germain meet. On the first floor is the small, timbered, tapestried Louis XIII salon whence you can look down from the breakfast table onto the bustle below. Most of the bedrooms are smallish and all give onto the streets, so it may be a tad noisy for the sensitive. There are bright floral fabrics, smart bottle-green carpeting, prettily tiled bathrooms. On the top floor you find sloping ceilings and beams: one bedroom is reached through its half-timbered bathroom.

Price	€76–€134.
Rooms	30 twins/doubles.
Meals	Breakfast €11.
Closed	Never.
Directions	Metro: St Germain des Prés (4), Mabillon (10), Odéon (4, 10).
	RER: St Michel-Notre Dame.
	Buses: 39, 48, 58, 63, 70, 86, 87, 95.
	Parking: St Germain des Prés, St Sulpice.

Madame Perrine Henneveux
66 rue de Seine, 75006 Paris

Tel	+33 (0)1 46 34 24 80
Web	www.welcomehotel-paris.com

Hôtel Prince de Conti

The narrow rue Guénégaud is one to savour slowly. The Prince de Conti – the Princess lived here in 1670 – feels as authentic the moment your feet hit the lobby's parquet floor. The choice is eclectic but it works: a comfy sofa in the bay window, a faïence stove, chinoiserie bamboo chairs, and a lovely bronze figure in movement watches all from its three-legged pedestal. If you are splurging, ask for the suite on the top floor with its antique desk, checked armchairs and double-sinked bathroom; the ground-level rooms open onto the interior courtyard. If you're on a budget, the smaller rooms on the courtyard will suit; ask for one with two windows.

Price	€150–€300.
Rooms	28: 21 doubles, 5 twins, 2 duplexes for 3.
Meals	Breakfast €13.
Closed	Never.
Directions	Metro: St Germain des Près (4), Odéon (4,10), Pont Neuf (7). RER: St Michel-Notre Dame. Buses: 58, 70. Parking: Rue Mazarine.

Hélène Touber
8 rue Guénégaud, 75006 Paris

Tel   +33 (0)1 44 07 30 40
Web   www.prince-de-conti.com

Hôtel de Seine

It still feels like a private mansion and the delightful welcome adds to this impression. There are two salons off the hall, fresh flowers, space, deep quiet. The breakfast room has a large table for the sociable and several small tables for the less so; walls are clothed in Florentine-style fabric. Bedrooms have class too, with strong colour schemes, furniture that is gently painted Louis XVI or highly polished. Most rooms have quirky layouts dictated by the old architecture. The higher floors naturally carry 18th-century timbers and the occasional balcony for rooftop views or birds-eye vistas. A good place to stay.

Price	€195–€205. Singles €175. Triples €230.
Rooms	30: 14 doubles, 8 twins, 4 singles, 4 triples.
Meals	Breakfast €12–€13.
Closed	Never.
Directions	Metro: St Germain des Prés (4), Mabillon (10), Odéon (4, 10). RER: St Michel-Notre Dame. Buses: 39, 48, 58, 63, 70, 86, 87, 95. Parking: Rue Mazarine.

Madame Perrine Henneveux
52 rue de Seine, 75006 Paris

Tel	+33 (0)1 46 34 22 80
Web	www.hoteldeseine.com

Hôtel Saint Germain des Prés

There are two spirits afloat in Saint Germain. And because it sometimes feels that the bright-and-blinky has the upper hand, one seeks quiet reminders of another time, like the Place de Furstenberg with Delacroix's museum. Or take a room here, where the time button has hit pause. Be seduced by the pale translucent beauty of the Murano chandelier in reception, and the antique tapestry. The salon/breakfast room is lit by a glass wall, with a winter garden and a painted mural, theatrically draped and framed. Bedrooms are in the same mode with a boudoir feel and beams galore. Bathrooms are proper 21st century. Amazing.

Price	€170–€290. Single €130. Suites €350.
Rooms	30: 27 twins/doubles, 1 single, 2 suites for 2.
Meals	Buffet breakfast €10.
Closed	Never.
Directions	Metro: St Germain des Prés (4). RER: St Michel-Notre Dame. Buses: 39, 48, 63, 86, 87, 95. Parking: 169 Boulevard St Germain.

Eric Desfaudais
36 rue Bonaparte, 75006 Paris

Tel	+33 (0)1 43 26 00 19
Web	www.hotel-paris-saint-germain.com

Hôtel de Buci

At the heart of the little shopping streets behind St Germain, the Buci feels like another antique shop, full of beautiful pieces. In the salon every picture is worth a good look and every portrait is intriguing. Come evening, the music turns to jazz to fit the 1930s atmosphere and in the basement piano bar/breakfast space, you can sit on superbly ornate red sofas. Bedrooms have good repro furniture and remarkable fabrics from top design houses: sun yellow and redcurrant, cornflower blue and cream, checks, stripes and florals in a rich coordination of canopies, pelmets and quilts. A good, reliable and quiet place.

Price	€195–€335. Suites €330–€550.
Rooms	24: 12 doubles, 8 twins, 4 suites for 3-4.
Meals	Breakfast €17–€22.
Closed	Never.
Directions	Metro: St Germain des Prés (4), Mabillon (10). RER: St Michel-Notre Dame. Buses: 58 70. Parking: St Germain des Prés.

Christophe Falaise
22 rue Buci, 75006 Paris

Tel	+33 (0)1 55 42 74 74
Web	www.buci-hotel.com

Entry 50 Map 8

Artus Hôtel

Attitude and plenty of it. The Artus has attracted a young, trendy art crowd who would stay at no other place. You pass two stunning primitive statues displayed in the large windows on the street, then a sweep of an entrance leads you past the slim reception desk and into a cluster of bright bucket chairs. It is all rather fresh and breathless. The challenge here is space: the rooms were never big so functionality mixed with style is what counts. The final touch is the artistic detail in every room. Leather trims, red silk curtains, Murano basins, open bathrooms with smoked green glass, tweed curtains; it's refreshing and new.

Price	€195-€305. Suite & duplex €395-€415.
Rooms	27: 20 doubles, 5 twins, 1 suite for 2, 1 duplex.
Meals	Buffet breakfast included.
Closed	Never.
Directions	Metro: St Germain des Prés (4), Mabillon (10), Odéon (4,10). RER: St Michel-Notre Dame. Buses: 58, 63, 70, 86, 87, 96. Parking: St Germain des Prés.

Christophe Falaise
34 rue de Buci, 75006 Paris

Tel	+33 (0)1 43 29 07 20
Web	www.artushotel.com

Hôtel d'Aubusson

Go through the superb old doors into the flagstoned hall – hear the quiet piano, see the fountained magnificence through the patio doors – and relax. It is a beautiful stone building, serene and elegant in its 17th-century proportions, properly modern in its renovation. Reading by the great hearth or breakfasting in the Aubusson-hung room beyond, you are cocooned in pure French style. There are two lovely patios for summer drinks, a luxurious bar with piano entertainment in the evenings. Bedrooms are big or very big, all richly, unfussily furnished. A grand, peaceful house where guests are nurtured by friendly staff.

Price	€255-€450. Suite €535. Duplexes €480.
Rooms	50: 46 doubles, 1 suite, 3 duplexes.
Meals	Breakfast: wake-up €7, buffet €23.
	Light meals with wine, from €39.
Closed	Never.
Directions	Metro: Odéon.
	RER: St Michel-Notre Dame, Pont-Neuf.
	Buses: 56, 63, 70, 86, 87, 96.
	Parking: At hotel.

Monsieur Walter Waeterloos
33 rue Dauphine, 75006 Paris

Tel	+33 (0)1 43 29 43 43
Web	www.hoteldaubusson.com

Entry 52 Map 8

Millésime Hôtel

"Our room had an impossible peacefulness – all I could hear was constant birdsong" (a reader). Behind its imposing old doors, the Millésime is intimate, pretty, quiet and welcoming. There are deep sofas set on glowing parquet and a charming patio for summer breakfasts. Bedrooms, with pale yellow walls, contemporary checks and good white and grey bathrooms, vary in size but are never too cramped. At the top, two rooms with brilliant high-peaked ceilings and roof windows over historic towers and domes; at the bottom a vaulted breakfast room. Spic and span after a renovation in 2008, this is good value in a superb location.

Price	€190–€220. Suite €380.
Rooms	21: 20 doubles, 1 suite.
Meals	Breakfast €13–€16.
Closed	Never.
Directions	Metro: St Germain des Prés. RER: St Michel-Notre Dame. Buses: 39, 48, 63, 86, 95. Parking: St Germain des Prés.

Julien Lucas
15 rue Jacob, 75006 Paris

Tel	+33 (0)1 44 07 97 97
Web	www.millesimehotel.com

Hôtel des Deux Continents

The hotel and its three ancient listed buildings sit among the decorating and antique shops. Its public rooms are hugely atmospheric with fresh flowers, beams, gilt frames. Venus stands shyly among the greenery on the patio and tables are laid with fine white cloths. Two buildings look onto quiet inner courtyards, the larger, noisier rooms are at the front. Some rooms have rooftop views, some look onto flowered terraces, all contemporary-classic in style in occasionally surprising mixtures of colours but it all 'works'. The smallest rooms are utterly quiet and equally charming. Masses of personality and young and welcoming staff.

Price	€124-€185. Singles €101-€165. Triples €185-€230.
Rooms	41: 19 doubles, 10 twins, 8 singles, 4 triples.
Meals	Breakfast €11-€12.
Closed	Never.
Directions	Metro: St Germain des Prés (4).
	RER B: St Michel Notre-Dame.
	Buses: 39, 48, 58, 63, 70, 86, 87, 95,

Madame Perrine Henneveux
25 rue Jacob, 75006 Paris

Tel	+33 (0)1 43 26 72 46
Web	www.hoteldes2continents.com

La Villa Saint Germain

Soft silky curtains the colour of glazed chestnuts, curvy steel stair rail, ochre-flecked stone floor slabs; gentle music, deep chairs in grey, brown and café latte plush on a teak floor by the bar. In the bedrooms, more drama of colour and rich and yielding materials — silk-lined curtain, 'crocodile'-skin bedheads in dark wooden frames against scarlet walls, fluffy white duvets with dark grey and ivory woollen squares on top. And the details: room numbers light-projected in front of the door, monogrammed linen, superb designer bathrooms in chrome and ground glass, big stone-framed mirrors.

Price	€285-€370. Suites €470.
Rooms	31: 17 doubles, 10 twins, 4 suites for 2.
Meals	Continental breakfast €16, buffet €22.
Closed	Never.
Directions	Metro: St Germain des Prés (4), Mabillon (10). RER: St Michel-Notre Dame. Buses: 39, 48, 58, 63, 70, 86, 95, 96. Parking: St Germain des Prés.

♿ ✉ 📶 🚴

Christine Horbette
29 rue Jacob, 75006 Paris

Tel	+33 (0)1 43 26 60 00
Web	www.villa-saintgermain.com

Entry 55 Map 8

Hôtel du Danube

Built in the 1870s as a private mansion, this soft, civilised hotel rejoices in a dazzling black and red salon and a pale salmon patio where potted palms and a spreading rhododendron sit on quadrangles of teak and stone. Tables can be laid here for breakfast and elegant façades rise skywards. Croissants are also served in the light, airy breakfast room off the patio, where a delightful collection of blue china teapots sits on lighted shelves. The quietest rooms look over the patio or the smaller lightwell with its pretty trompe-l'oeil skyscape. Superb 'superior' rooms have two windows, high ceilings, big closets, some very desirable antiques, armchairs and smart fabrics.

Price	€148–€235. Family rooms & suite €245.
Rooms	40: 28 doubles, 9 twins, 2 family rooms, 1 suite.
Meals	Breakfast €11.
Closed	Never.
Directions	Metro: St Germain des Prés (4).
	RER: Musée d'Orsay.
	Buses: 39, 48, 63, 95, 96.
	Parking: St Germain des Prés.

Michel Sario
58 rue Jacob, 75006 Paris

Tel	+33 (0)1 42 60 34 70
Web	www.hoteldanube.fr

Entry 56 Map 8

Hôtel Lenox Saint Germain

The Lenox Club bar is used by publishers for drinks after work, by film stars for interviews, by writers for literary wrangles... utterly St Germain des Prés, great fun. The whole place has been transformed into a symphony of pure 1930s style and large bedrooms and (much) smaller ones are all different; some have old furniture, some have modern units. Rooms on the little rue du Pré aux Clercs are quieter and you may have the added luxury of a balcony. We really like the corner rooms with two windows and lots of light. You breakfast in a vaulted basement room, looked after by friendly staff who make you feel you belong.

Price	€140-€180. Suites €230-€330.
Rooms	34: 17 doubles, 12 twins, 5 suites.
Meals	Breakfast €11-€14. Bar snacks €5-€10. Wine €5.
Closed	Never.
Directions	Metro: St Germain des Prés (4), Rue du Bac (12). RER: Musée d'Orsay. Buses: 48, 39, 63, 68, 69, 83, 94. Parking: Rue des Saints Pères, Rue du Bac.

Madame Laporte
9 rue de l'Université, 75007 Paris
Tel   +33 (0)1 42 96 10 95
Web   www.lenoxsaintgermain.com

St Germain des Prés – Orsay

Hôtel Bourgogne et Montana

Luxury of the four-star variety has now taken over the whole of this marvellous hotel. The owner's grandfather, a bored MP in the 1890s, drew the wicked caricatures; his own antiques and pictures are placed for your pleasure in the famous raspberry rotunda, the primrose salon and the deeply tempting breakfast room that is full of light and the most sinful buffet (included in the price). Abandon yourself to the caress of fine damask, Jouy and deep velvet. The bigger rooms and suites have space and antiques and some extraordinary bathrooms with Italian tiles; the smaller ones are like rich, embracing nests. *Children under 12 free.*

Price	€180–290. Singles €180–€200. Suites €360–€380.
Rooms	32: 23 twins/doubles, 3 singles, 6 suites.
Meals	Buffet breakfast included.
Closed	Never.
Directions	Metro: Assemblée Nationale (12), Invalides (8,13). RER & Air France bus: Invalides. Buses: 93, 83, 63. Parking: Invalides.

Christophe Falaise
3 rue de Bourgogne, 75007 Paris

Tel	+33 (0)1 45 51 20 22
Web	www.bourgogne-montana.com

Entry 58 Map 3

Duc de Saint Simon

If Lauren Bacall chose this jewel over the Ritz, there has got to be a good reason. Perhaps it was the hideaway feel, terrifically peaceful on a tiny street. Or perhaps it was the elegant cosiness of the salon, enveloped in an extraordinary pleated yellow and red fabric with swagged garlands. The Bacall 'suite' is pale yellows and puffy beige satins with a leafy view. The other rooms, four with private terraces, are not large but just as appealing in the originality of their décor and fabrics. Service is responsive and charming, and it's no problem at all if you arrive early: a leisurely drink at one of the garden tables serenaded by birdsong will put you in the right mood.

Price	€225–€290. Suites €385–€395.
Rooms	34: 29 twins/doubles, 5 suites for 2.
Meals	Breakfast €15.
Closed	Never.
Directions	Metro: Rue du Bac (12). RER: St Michel–Notre Dame. Buses: 63, 68, 69, 83, 84, 94. Parking: Private parking available.

Gisela Siggelko
14 rue de Saint Simon, 75007 Paris

Tel	+33 (0)1 44 39 20 20
Web	www.hotelducdesaintsimon.com

Hôtel des Marronniers

A private-mansion hotel, it stands between quiet courtyard and real garden. The almost dramatically Second Empire salon, all ruches and gilt, leads to a delectable old-style conservatory where marble-topped tables await you under the fruity 'chandeliers', reflecting the big shrubby garden – privilege indeed. Rooms vary: mostly smallish, they all give onto the garden or front courtyard. The décor is based on coordinated fabrics, bright floral prints or Regency stripes serving as backdrop to an antique desk or a carved armoire. After so much light, the basement breakfast room is in soft, dark contrast for cool winter mornings.

Price	€149-€190. Singles €105-€135. Triple/quadruple €230-€250.
Rooms	37: 24 doubles, 8 twins, 3 singles, 1 triple, 1 quadruple.
Meals	Breakfast €12-€14.
Closed	Never.
Directions	Metro: St Germain des Prés (4). RER B: St Michel-Notre Dame. Buses: 39, 48, 63, 86, 95. Parking: St Germain des Prés.

Madame Perrine Henneveux
21 rue Jacob, 75006 Paris
Tel   +33 (0)1 43 25 30 60
Web   www.hoteldesmarronniers.com

Studio Eiffel

Between the monumental solemnity of the Invalides and the iconic airiness of the Eiffel Tower, the unfussy Studio Eiffel is well lit for a first floor with a leafy, birdy tree peering over the neighbour's wall. A good red-quilted bed on parquet flooring, pretty pieces of painted oriental furniture, an eating table between the two double windows and a proper fitted kitchen. The little shower room comes complete with pink towels and slippers. With nothing pretentious or over-studied, it is a neat and ideally central little space for putting your feet up after tramping from 15th-century church to 20th-century pyramid to ephemeral fashion house.

Price	€119; €750 per week.
Rooms	Twin/double studio. Shower room.
Meals	Restaurants nearby.
Closed	Never.
Directions	Directions on booking.

Valérie Zuber
155 rue de Grenelle, 75007 Paris
Tel   +33 (0)6 30 93 81 35

Entry 59 Map 3

10 rue Las Cases

In a provincial-quiet city street, classy dressed stone outside, intelligence, sobriety and style inside. Madame takes you into her vast, serene apartment: no modern gadgets or curly antiques, just a few good pieces, much space, and light-flooded parquet floors. Beyond the dining room, your cosy buff bedroom gives onto a big, silent, arcaded courtyard. Your hosts have lived all over the world, and Madame, as quiet and genuine as her surroundings, now enjoys her country garden near Chartres and the company of like-minded visitors – she is worth getting to know. *Minimum stay two nights preferred.*

Price	€85.
Rooms	1 twin/double.
Meals	Restaurants within walking distance.
Closed	Rarely.
Directions	Lift to 2nd floor.
	Metro: Solférino (12), Assemblée Nationale (12),
	Invalides (8).
	Parking: Invalides.

Élisabeth Marchal
75007 Paris

Tel   +33 (0)1 47 05 70 21

Hôtel de Varenne

Step into the little green cul de sac with its ivy-covered walls, hidden fountain and exquisite canopy over the entrance door and you have tumbled into an oasis of peace and calm. In the reception two bronze statues grace antique chests of drawers and a gilt-studded balustrade leads you upstairs. Most of the bedrooms look onto the quiet garden and most are a reasonable size for Paris. Monsieur Pommier is a man of detail and classic taste: in the bedrooms fabrics are carefully coordinated and good bathrooms have moulded basins. The four bigger rooms give onto the street. Charming staff work hard to make your stay special.

Price	€127–€197.
Rooms	24: 14 doubles, 10 twins.
Meals	Breakfast €10.
Closed	Never.
Directions	Metro: Varenne (13), Invalides (8, 13). RER & Air France bus: Invalides. Bus: 69. Parking: Invalides.

Jean-Marc Pommier
44 rue de Bourgogne, 75007 Paris
Tel   +33 (0)1 45 51 45 55
Web   www.hoteldevarenne.com

Entry 61 Map 3

Eiffel Park Hotel

What was once a shiny business hotel has been softened with Asian furniture and *objets*, oriental rugs and colonial armchairs. Pass a carved Indian gate to the small bar and salon with low-slung leather armchairs, then enter the Garcia-designed breakfast room. Most bedrooms reveal a rustic touch of the Far East in little chests and bedside tables. Rooms are not big but have some quirky shapes and angles, some have parquet floors, others toile de Jouy. The crowning glory is the roof terrace where grapes grow, lavender perfumes the air and you can breakfast under parasols. And there's home-grown honey for breakfast.

Price	€155–€290.
Rooms	35 twins/doubles.
Meals	Breakfast €15.
Closed	Never.
Directions	Metro: La Tour Maubourg. RER & Air France bus: Invalides.

Françoise Testard
17 bis rue Amélie, 75007 Paris
Tel   +33 (0)1 45 55 10 01
Web   www.eiffelpark.com

Entry 62 Map 3

Hôtel de Londres Eiffel

Halfway between 'La Grande Dame' (the Eiffel Tower) and the gilded lid over Napoleon's simple place of rest (he was less kindly known as the Little Corporal), here is a friendly, warm-coloured and warm-hearted hotel. The mixture of fine blinds and heavy curtains makes for a most welcoming atmosphere in the lobby and round into the sitting/breakfast area where lively fabric gaily wraps the chairs. Six bedrooms on two floors are in the *pavillon*: beds are in alcoves, white and beige flowers dress windows and good bath and shower rooms have well-lit wood-framed mirrors. You will be well looked after by Isabelle and her team.

Price	€110–€215. Singles €99–€165. Family room €250.
Rooms	30: 15 doubles, 7 twins, 7 singles, 1 family room for 3.
Meals	Breakfast €14.
Closed	Never.
Directions	Metro: Ecole Militaire.
	RER: Pont de l'Alma.
	Buses: 69, 80, 87.
	Parking: Ecole Militaire.

Isabelle Prigent
1 rue Augereau, 75007 Paris
Tel +33 (0)1 45 51 63 02
Web www.londres-eiffel.com

Hôtel Gavarni

The Gavarni heaves itself up into the miniature luxury class on ropes of rich draperies, heavenly bathrooms and superb finishes. The suites and doubles at the top are stunning with their massage shower panels, canopies and beautiful furniture – supremely French with Eiffel Tower views. The first four floors are less luxurious but the quality is the same. The triumph is those cramped little bathrooms which have gained so much space with their ingenious made-to-measure red 'granite' basin, shower and loo. A terrific organic, fairtrade breakfast is served on the patio; energy is renewable and only eco-friendly detergents are used.

Price	€160–€200. Singles €110–€170. Suites and family rooms €240–€500.
Rooms	25: 10 doubles, 6 twins, 4 singles, 5 family rooms for 3–4, 4 suites.
Meals	Breakfast €15.
Closed	Never.
Directions	Metro: Passy (6), Trocadéro (6, 9). RER: Boulainvilliers. Buses: 22, 32. Parking: Garage Moderne, Rue de Passy.

Xavier Moraga
5 rue Gavarni, 75116 Paris

Tel	+33 (0)1 45 24 52 82
Web	www.gavarni.com

Hôtel Passy Eiffel

When you step off the smart shopping street you can certainly believe that Passy was a little village 100 years ago. The atmosphere is calm and nothing is overdone. Lounge in the glassed-in veranda where you can see a gardener's cottage across the tiny cobbled yard. Two salons off the panelled hall give onto the street through arching windows. Rooms are decorated in floral quilts and curtains; the suite has four windows onto That Tower, blue moiré walls, a sofabed in the sitting area, a pretty period desk. Beams and timbers frame the upper floors; on the courtyard side, you look onto the hotel's patio and the neighbour's lovely garden.

Price	€160–€185. Family rooms & suites €210–€250.
Rooms	49: 40 twins/doubles, 5 singles, 2 family rooms for 3, 2 suites for 2.
Meals	Breakfast €14.
Closed	Never.
Directions	Metro: Passy (6).
	RER: Boulainvilliers.
	Buses: 22, 32.
	Parking: 19 rue de Passy.

	Christine Horbette
	10 rue de Passy, 75016 Paris
Tel	+33 (0)1 45 25 55 66
Web	www.passyeiffel.com

HotelHome Paris 16

A flat in Paris – with a difference. In this quiet street in a classic 1900s building, Laurence combines hotel services with a family-like atmosphere. A glass roof runs across a narrow courtyard lush with fern, jasmine and honeysuckle – perfect for leisurely breakfast. The tiniest lift in Paris will get your bags up or down to the big rooms, each with a salon and a fabulous customised kitchenette. Charming are the marble fireplaces and antique radiators; modern are the ochre walls, bright rugs and plaid armchairs. Big apartments at the top have two or three bedrooms; smaller rooms on the ground floor have garden views. *Mention you are from Sawday's for a special price.*

Price	€175–€460.
Rooms	17 apartments: 5 for 2-3, 10 for 4, 2 for 6.
Meals	Restaurants within walking distance.
Closed	Rarely.
Directions	Metro: Jasmin (9).
	RER: Boulainvilliers.
	Buses: 22, 52.
	Parking: Some private parking, enquire at hotel.

	Laurence Vivant
	36 rue George Sand, 75016 Paris
Tel	+33 (0)1 45 20 61 38
Web	www.hotelhome.fr

Entry 66 Map 6

11 rue de Siam

A vivacious, much-travelled photographer, Anne has her eyrie up a small private stair in the upper-class peace of Passy where she lays breakfast for you in her pretty kitchen with the Eiffel Tower view. In your elegant, atmospheric suite where sitting and sleeping sections connect, you'll find oriental draperies, family antiques and a window to the quiet white courtyard. In the sitting room, masses of art books, paintings, a piano and photographs, all superb illustrations of Anne's interests and fascinating travellers tales, told in fluent English. And she's full of insights into what's on in Paris. *Minimum stay two nights. German & Italian spoken.*

Price	€100–€110. Extra person €20.
Rooms	1 suite for 2-3, sharing bathroom.
Meals	Restaurants within walking distance.
Closed	Rarely.
Directions	Metro: Rue de la Pompe (9). RER: Henri Martin. Buses: 63, 52.

Anne de Henning
75116 Paris

Tel   +33 (0)1 45 04 50 06

Hôtel Keppler

A top-class hotel with all the bells and whistles in one of the ritziest parts of Paris, nicely near the Champs-Elysées yet far enough away to hear your own footsteps on the small side street. The bedrooms are outstanding and the basic black and white theme is splashed with a touch or two of mauve, chinese red or sun yellow as counterpoints. Thick white damask curtains contrast nicely with dark leather headboards and plaid bedcovers. There is a glass canopied salon and an architectural feat of daylight and garden in the open-sided breakfast space downstairs. Alain Lagarrigue is at the helm and a warm welcome is guaranteed.

Price	€265–€490. Suites €475–€1,000.
Rooms	39: 34 twins/doubles, 4 suites, 1 suite for 4.
Meals	Buffet breakfast €22.
Closed	Never.
Directions	Metro: Charles de Gaulle-Étoile.
	RER & Air France bus: Charles de Gaulle-Étoile.
	Buses: 22, 32, 73, 92.
	Parking: Avenue Marceau.

	Alain Lagarrigue
	10 rue Kepler, 75116 Paris
Tel	+33 (0)1 47 20 65 05
Web	www.keppler.fr

Étoile – Champs-Élysées

Hotel

Hôtel François 1er

Period furniture, lamps and pictures in a brilliant mix of classic, baroque and contemporary – all brought together by Alain Lagarrigue whose spirit infuses the whole house. The salon and bar areas are intimate and panelled; a glassed-in patio with year-round greenery, a Turkish rug on parquet, real books on coffee tables and faux books around the bar summon you to comfort and ease. Alain prides himself on the well-kept rooms and rich fabrics; those stretched on the walls match the patterns on the fine beds. Some are incredible jewel boxes of intense poppy reds or elegant pale yellows and the tropical breakfast room is a joy.

Price	€350–€490. Suite €800–€1,000.
Rooms	40: 39 twins/doubles, 1 suite.
Meals	Breakfast €21.
Closed	Never.
Directions	Metro: George V (1).
	RER & Air France bus: Charles de Gaulle-Étoile.
	Buses: 22, 32, 73, 92.
	Parking: George V.

Alain Lagarrigue
7 rue Magellan, 75008 Paris

Tel	+33 (0)1 47 23 44 04
Web	www.the-paris-hotel.com

Entry 69 Map 3

1 rue Lamennais

Even the air feels quietly elegant. Soisick uses no frills, just good things old and new:
the sense of peace is palpable (nothing to do with double glazing). Her flat turns away
from the rowdy Champs-Élysées towards classy St Honoré: ask this gentle Parisian for
advice about great little restaurants – or anything Parisian. The simple generous
bedroom has size and interest – an unusual inlaid table is set off by white bedcovers –
and leads to a dressing room fit for a star and your tasteful white and grey bathroom.
With three windows, parquet floor and its mix of antique and modern, the living
room is another charmer.

Price	€90.
Rooms	1 twin/double.
Meals	Restaurants nearby.
Closed	Rarely.
Directions	Metro: George V (1), Charles de Gaulle-Étoile (1, 2, 6). RER & Air France bus: Charles de Gaulle-Étoile. Buses: 22, 30, 31, 52, 73, 92, 93, Balabus. Parking: Étoile.

Soisick Guérineau
75008 Paris
Tel   +33 (0)1 40 39 04 38

Hôtel des Champs-Élysées

The centrepiece of recent renovations here is Madame's amazing collection of hat pins lovingly displayed in the main lobby. A warning however: check in first because you will certainly get caught up in these beautiful pieces and may never make it up to your room! Don't worry, photos of some of the more outstanding ones are featured over the beds. Like the hat pins, the rooms are not big but each is beautiful: luscious, beaded taffeta curtains in swirly patterns replace doors to bathrooms; silver wallpaper and grey metallic headboards shimmer, bronze bedcovers glow and chocolate carpeting muffles every sound.

Price	€120–€365.
Rooms	26 doubles.
Meals	Breakfast €18.
Closed	Never.
Directions	Metro: St Philippe du Roule (9), Franklin Roosevelt (1, 9). RER & Air France bus: Charles de Gaulle-Étoile. Buses: 22, 28, 32, 73, 80, 83, 93. Parking: Rue de Ponthieu.

Marie-Joëlle Monteil
2 rue d'Artois, 75008 Paris

Tel   +33 (0)1 43 59 11 42
Web   www.champselysees-paris-hotel.com

Entry 71 Map 3

Hôtel Pergolèse

Once past the blue doors you forget the trumpeting sculptures of nearby Arc de Triomphe for a festival of modern design. Édith Vidalenc works with designer Rena Dumas, creator of Hermès boutiques, to keep a sleek but warm, human hotel. Her sense of hospitality informs it all. Pastel tones are mutedly smart so the multi-coloured breakfast room is a slightly humorous wake-up call, the linen and fine silver a bow to tradition. Rooms are all furnished in pale wood and leather, thick curtains and soft white bedcovers. The star, *Pergolèse*, is a small masterpiece in palest apricot with spots of colour and a superb open bathroom.

Price	€175–€290. Suite €270–€390.
Rooms	40: 36 doubles (some interconnect), 3 singles, 1 suite.
Meals	Breakfast €12–€18.
Closed	Never.
Directions	Metro: Argentine (1). RER A: Charles de Gaulle-Étoile; RER C: Porte Maillot. Air France bus: Porte Maillot. Parking: Avenue Foch/Porte Maillot.

Édith Vidalenc
3 rue Pergolèse, 75116 Paris

Tel   +33 (0)1 53 64 04 04
Web   www.parishotelpergolese.com

Entry 72 Map 2

Hôtel de Banville

Deliciously Parisian, the Banville has the elegance of inherited style and the punch of ultra-modern fittings. You feel welcomed into a private château where gilt-edged Old Masters supervise the gracious salon with its grand piano (the owner sings on Tuesday nights). The designs are wondrous and fairy-lit. *Marie*, in subtle tones from palest eggshell to rich red loam, has a canopied bed, a little terrace (Eiffel Tower view) and a brilliant bathroom with thick curtains for soft partitioning; the three *Pastourelles* are freshly countrified in gingham. Staff are delightful – hospitality could have been born here. *Chauffeur for airport pick-up & private tours arranged.*

Price	€310–€420.
Rooms	38: 37 twins/doubles, 1 suite.
Meals	Breakfast €20. Light meals €20–€30. Wine €6.
Closed	Never.
Directions	Metro: Porte de Champerret (3), Pereire (3). RER: Pereire. Buses: 92, 84, 93. Parking: Rue de Courcelles.

Marianne Moreau
166 boulevard Berthier, 75017 Paris

Tel	+33 (0)1 42 67 70 16
Web	www.hotelbanville.fr

Entry 73 Map 2

New Orient Hôtel

People come to this area of Paris from over the world with their violins, guitars and lutes and the New Orient, pretty, original and fun sits among all the musicians. The warm, attractive owners love country-house sales and the mixed styles they've collected co-exist harmoniously. There are brass beds and carved beds, an inlaid dressing table, a marble washstand and, everywhere, oriental or Mediterranean fabrics. On the ground floor, a painted telephone box, a carved dresser, a piano and, in the breakfast area, a grandfather clock. A thoroughly characterful place with the nicest people possible at the helm. We like it a lot.

Price	€120–€160. Singles €95.
Rooms	30: 12 doubles, 8 twins, 10 singles.
Meals	Breakfast €11.
Closed	Never.
Directions	Metro: Villiers (2, 3), Europe (3). RER & Roissybus: Auber, Opéra. Buses: 30, 53. Parking: Europe.

Catherine & Sepp Wehrlé
16 rue de Constantinople, 75008 Paris
Tel   +33 (0)1 45 22 21 64
Web   www.hotelneworient.com

Côté Montmartre

Walk in and touch an 1890s heart: floral inlay on the stairs, stained-glass windows behind the lift. On the top landing, a curly bench greets you. Young and quietly smiling, Isabelle leads you to her personality-filled living room, a harmony of family antiques and 20th-century design, and a gift of a view: old Paris crookedly climbing to the Sacré Cœur. Breakfast may be on the flowering balcony, perhaps with fat cat Jules. Your big white (no-smoking) bedroom off the landing is modern and new-bedded in peaceful rooftop seclusion; the shower room a contemporary jewel. Interesting, cultured, cosmopolitan people, too.

Price	€130–€150. Child's bed available €30.
Rooms	1 double.
Meals	Restaurants nearby.
Closed	Rarely.
Directions	Metro: Trinité (12), Pigalle (2, 12). Buses: 26, 43, 67, 68, 73, 81, 85. RER: Auber.

Isabelle & Jacques Bravo
11 bis rue Jean Baptiste Pigalle, 75009 Paris

Tel	+33 (0)1 43 54 33 09
Web	www.cotemontmartre.com

Hôtel Langlois – Croisés

Built as a bank in 1870, the best rooms in this splendid building are rich in wood and detail: ceramic and marble fireplaces, superbly crafted cupboards, carved alcoves. They are big enough too to take heavy velvet and deep colours, and many have equally generous bathrooms. In the attractive breakfast room there's a lovely antique birdcage. Madame Bojena, a gentle and efficient presence, is deeply protective of the building's history and structure and has collected furniture and sculpture to suit. Take the stairs and admire the fine paintings on the landings. There's double glazing but the traffic does die down after 8pm.

Price	€140–€150. Suites €190.
Rooms	27: 19 doubles, 5 twins, 3 suites for 3-4.
Meals	Breakfast €13.
Closed	Never.
Directions	Metro: Trinité-d'Estienne d'Orves (12). RER & Roissybus: Auber, Opéra. Buses: 26, 32, 42, 43, 68, 81. Parking: Parking 300m, enquire at hotel.

Madame Bojena
63 rue St Lazare, 75009 Paris
Tel   +33 (0)1 48 74 78 24
Web   www.hotel-langlois.com

Entry 76 Map 3

Hôtel La Sanguine

Through a little lobby and up one flight to a house of easy friendliness. Delightful, energetic people and Tokyo, the sausage dog, welcome you. A couple of classical statues overlook the breakfast tables and a little patio: hard to believe that the powers of this world – ministers, fashion gurus, ambassadors – live round the corner. Rooms have good discreet personality. Your hosts make your breakfast jam with orchard fruits; Monsieur bakes your croissant then irons your monogrammed towels; Madame is full of good advice on what to do. Excellent. *Wines and champagne sold for private consumption. No lift, 4 floors.*

Price	€99–€150. Family room €190.
Rooms	31: 17 doubles, 5 twins, 8 singles, 1 family room for 3.
Meals	Breakfast €13.
Closed	Never.
Directions	Metro: Madeleine (8, 12, 14), Concorde (1, 8, 12), Opéra (3,7), Auber (8). RER & Roissybus: Auber, Opéra. Buses: 42, 52, 84, 94. Parking: Madeleine, Concorde.

Entry 77 Map 3

Monsieur & Madame Plumerand
6 rue de Surène, 75008 Paris
Tel   +33 (0)1 42 65 71 61
Web   www.hotel-la-sanguine.com

Le Relais Madeleine

If you are wondering where in Paris you can you relax in a warm bubbly tub and catch up on your favourite TV program, go no further, the brand new Relais Madeleine has thought of that and just about everything else you would have had in mind for a perfect stay. There is a delightful patio, a room with a sauna and terrace, a marvelous suite for four on the top floor, all carefully decorated in warm, floral fabrics, excellent pieces of furniture, top mattresses and the softest linens. This charming little street is a perfect balance between the business district and pleasant shopping areas around the Opéra and the Madeleine.

Price	€175–€255. Suite €450.
Rooms	23: 21 doubles, 1 single, 1 suite.
Meals	Breakfast €13.
Closed	Never.
Directions	Metro: Madeleine.
	RER & Roissybus: Auber.

Paul Bogaert
11 bis rue Godot de Mauroy, 75009 Paris

Tel	+33 (0)1 47 42 22 40
Web	www.relaismadeleine.fr

Entry 78 Map 3

Hôtel Massena

One of our favourite streets, backed at one end by the Byzantine cupola of the ever-humming Galeries Lafayette, and the Madeleine church with its Greek temple façade at the other. It is short, and blessed with fine trees, interesting fashion boutiques and cafés. The young, new owner is working her way through the hotel with style and verve. The lobby has already received a full, luminous vamp somewhere between the playful and the grownup with silver and pink on walls. Rooms are small but good and have space-saving sliding bathroom doors. The staff are friendly and there's a top-floor room with a terrace big enough to breakfast on.

Price	€155–€160. Family rooms €160–€250.
Rooms	36: 21 doubles, 8 twins, 5 family rooms for 3, 2 family rooms for 4.
Meals	Breakfast €13.
Closed	Never.
Directions	Metro: Madeleine (8, 12, 14), Havre–Caumartin (9). RER & Roissybus: Auber, Opéra. Buses: 24, 42, 52, 84, 94. Parking: Madeleine.

Karine de Lapasse
16 rue Tronchet, 75008 Paris

Tel	+33 (0)1 47 42 71 22
Web	www.paris-hotel-massena.com

Hôtel Opéra Richepanse

The marquetry, the panelling, the smooth leather furniture and the stylish mouldings of the lobby-salon were all custom-designed for the deep renovations done by the owner. Bedrooms are a good size, some are enormous, the suites magnificent. They have clean-limbed polished 1930s-style furniture and excellent thick-textured fabrics for straight-hung curtains and well-fitting bedcovers – no swags, no frills, no fuss. Bathrooms are superb, with the latest in basin design, triple bevelled mirrors and simple, smart tiling. Modern comforts, old-style attention and service. *Room service from bistro next door.*

Price	€250-€440. Suites €460-€590.
Rooms	38: 35 twins/doubles, 3 suites.
Meals	Breakfast €13-€18.
Closed	Never.
Directions	Metro: Madeleine (8, 12, 14), Concorde (1, 12). RER & Roissybus: Auber, Opéra. Buses: 42, 52, 84, 94. Parking: Madeleine.

	Édith Vidalenc
	14 rue du Chevalier de St George, 75001 Paris
Tel	+33 (0)1 42 60 36 00
Web	www.richepanse.com

Hôtel Relais Montmartre

There are good reasons why artists still live in this village tucked in behind the Sacré Cœur, so book into this little jewel and the secrets of this 'rediscovered' neighbourhood will be revealed. Just up from *Amélie*'s celebrated café, in a tiny side street, the entrance is discreet. Elegance and intimacy blend in the lobby with fireplace and antique desk; the sofa, the period chairs and the curtains are an extraordinary mix of rich fabric; the small patio set with sunny yellow garden furniture is the cherry on the cake. Lovely bedrooms decorated with care, dreamy mattresses, attentive staff: simple luxury at its best.

Price	€160-€200.
Rooms	26 doubles.
Meals	Breakfast €13.
Closed	Never.
Directions	Metro: Blanche (2), Place de Clichy (13, 2), Abbesses (12). RER: Gare du Nord. Buses: 30, 54, 80, 95. Parking: Private parking, enquire at hotel.

Paul Bogaert
6 rue Constance, 75018 Paris

Tel	+33 (0)1 70 64 25 25
Web	www.relaismontmartre.fr

Hôtel des Arts

Step off the steep narrow street into a big reception space, to Caramel, a big, friendly Lab, oriental rugs, long glass-fronted oak bookcase, old stones and smiling faces. On the right, a French-bourgeois salon with family antiques, interesting pictures, Provençal chairs and peace. Rooms are a reasonable size and in the same vein: simple and uncluttered, with good colour schemes. Some bathrooms have been renovated in crazy mosaic tiling, others are fine in their older beige garb. All the paintings are by Montmartre artists and the basement breakfast area where an excellent cold buffet is laid out is almost a gallery. Great value.

Price	€110. Singles €85.
Rooms	50: 33 doubles, 14 twins, 3 singles.
Meals	Buffet breakfast €10.
Closed	Never.
Directions	Metro: Blanche (2), Abbesses (12).
	RER: Gare du Nord.
	Buses: 30, 54, 68, 74, 80, Montmartrobus.
	Parking: Impasse Marie Blanche.

Philippe Lameyre
5 rue Tholozé, 75018 Paris

Tel	+33 (0)1 46 06 30 52	
Web	www.arts-hotel-paris.com	

Entry 82 Map 4

Terrass Hotel

The Terrass is the biggest (and highest) hotel in this book but the atmosphere is genuinely warm. Antiques and tapestries, bronzes and old prints remove any sense of cold grandeur and a pianist plays every evening. The breakfast buffet is a masterpiece in a room flooded with light; the chef has an excellent reputation and you may have the fine-weather privilege of eating on the 7th-floor terrace looking across the city. The suites are superb: big and light with windows that take in the greenery of Montmartre cemetery; other rooms have less space but all sport delectable colours and exude a sense of taste and attention to detail.

Price	€280–€330. Suites €380–€410.
Rooms	98: 83 twins/doubles, 15 suites.
Meals	Breakfast €17. Dinner from €23. Restaurant closed Sunday evenings.
Closed	Never.
Directions	Metro: St Lazare, Gare du Nord. Buses: 80, 95.

Entry 83 Map 3

Sabine Müller
12-14 rue Joseph de Maistre, 75018 Paris
Tel   +33 (0)1 46 06 72 85
Web   www.terrass-hotel.com

11 rue Duhesme

If you want a secret place for two with all mod cons in genuine old Paris, come here. The entrance, yard and stairs are authentically unprettified but when you reach the third floor you find a simple little gem with 1920s Paris sparkle. Old panelling and polished floors set the warm tone; the cast-iron fireplace sports new-style candles for evening glamour on the Récamier daybed, big letters on the wall spell out AMOUR. And the super-duper frothy white and blue bedroom is romantissimo. The whole place is deeply pleasing, has little luxuries such as Jo Malone smellies and bathrobes and a neat little kitchen. Exceptional.

Price	£595 per week.
Rooms	1 double, separate wc.
Meals	Restaurants nearby.
Closed	Never.
Directions	Directions on booking.

Brendan Kirwan
& Amanda Swanwick-Aharoni
75018 Paris

Mobile   +44 (0)7725 056421
Web   www.swell-apartments.co.uk

Entry 84 Map 7

Montmartre

Montmartre district

In Montmartre village, between busty boulevard and pure-white Sacré Cœur, barrister Valérie and her architect husband offer a super-chic and ideally autonomous studio off their charming, pot-planted and cobbled courtyard with your bistro table and chairs. A bed dressed in delicate red against white walls, an antique oval dining table, a pine-and-steel gem of a corner kitchen, a generous shower, a mirror framed in red. Valérie's discreet decorative flourishes speak for her calm, positive personality and her interest in other lands. A delicious Paris hideaway you can call your own. *Minimum stay three nights.*

Price	€100; €650 per week.
Rooms	1 studio for 2 & kitchenette.
Meals	Breakfast not included. Restaurants nearby.
Closed	Rarely.
Directions	Metro: Anvers Sacre Coeur (2).
	Metro/RER: Gare du Nord.
	Buses: 30, 31, 54, 85.
	Parking: Rue Fentrier.

Valérie Zuber
75018 Paris
Tel +33 (0)6 30 93 81 35

Belleville district

Sabine, artist and art therapist, "feeds people with colours". Jules makes the organic bread with a dazzling smile, and big, beautiful Taquin, his guide dog, loves people. Kindly and artistic, they live calmly in this bit of genuine old Paris between two tiny gardens and a tall house. The simple guest room, with good double bed and flame-covered sleigh-bed divan, a welcome tea-maker and an old-fashioned bathroom, shares a building with Sabine's studio. Healthfoody continental breakfast is in the cosy family room in the main house or outside under the birdsung tree. Such peace in Paris is rare.
Minimum stay two nights.

Price	€70.
Rooms	1 family room for 3.
Meals	Restaurants within walking distance.
Closed	July–August.
Directions	Metro: Jourdain (11), Place des Fêtes (11). Buses: 26, 48, 60. Parking: Place des Fêtes.

Sabine & Jules Aïm
75019 Paris

Tel   +33 (0)1 42 08 23 71

29 rue Belleville

The street throbs with multicultural motley but from the top of this clean modern block you can stretch your eyes across Paris to the scintillating towers of La Défense or round to the Parc de Belleville, a surprising green hillside above the city. Your pretty room lets in fabulous sunsets over the Eiffel Tower and no noise. The flat is all white walls, modern parquet floors and fine old family furniture, lots from Provence where your very proper, elderly hostess used to live. Madame serves fresh pastries at breakfast and tells you all about everything with great verve. *Minimum stay two nights. Spanish spoken.*

Price	€73.
Rooms	1 double.
Meals	Restaurants within walking distance.
Closed	Rarely.
Directions	Lift to 9th floor. Metro: Belleville (2, 11). Parking: ask owners.

Danièle de la Brosse
75019 Paris

Tel	+33 (0)1 42 41 99 59
Web	www.fleursdesoleil.fr/crans-maisons/75-delabrosse.htm

Entry 87 Map 5

Les Jardins de Marie

A big modern block and a fine old-style French welcome. Ground-floor rooms look out to communal gardens where birds sing among the lilac; the Bois de Vincennes is a walk away, Bastille reachable along the old railway line. Marie loves having guests and welcomes you easily to her unpretentious family room. Gérard was a biscuit engraver – the engraver's tables will intrigue you, as will the metal biscuit moulds turned into lamps. Pretty, colourful, comfortable bedrooms give onto the peace of the back garden. Walk the Coulée Verte to Bastille, ride the 87 bus for an almost-free view of historic Paris sights and return to the quiet garden.

Price	€90.
Rooms	3: 1 double with separate shower room & wc; 1 twin/double, 1 family room for 3, sharing separate bathroom.
Meals	Restaurants nearby.
Closed	Never.
Directions	Metro: Michel Bizot (8). RER: Gare de Lyon. Buses: 46, 87.

Marie-Hélène Chanat
46 rue de Fécamp, 75012 Paris

Tel	+33 (0)1 40 19 06 40
Web	www.aparisbnb.com

Entry 88 Map 9

Neuilly Studio

Neuilly is seen as either an honorary 21st arrondissement or the most urban-chic of suburbs: you are in the city but not of it. Your studio flat has a good square white room with an easily-manageable sofabed and windows that give onto a little garden. You enter your den via a diminutive kitchenette (fridge, kettle, induction hotplate, microwave) to find bookshelves, a big writing table and a cultured atmosphere. A journalist and singer of Russian origin, the owner greets you, observed by her ginger cat and her daughter's dog. Privacy, peace, easy transport and a high-class residential atmosphere: a special place indeed. *Enquire about B&B. Minimum stay two nights.*

Price	€85–€115 per day.
Rooms	Studio room with sofabed & kitchenette; bathroom.
Meals	Restaurants within walking distance.
Closed	Rarely.
Directions	Directions on booking.

Catherine Galitzine
92200 Neuilly sur Seine

Tel   +33 (0)1 47 22 91 14

Entry 89 Map 2

Le Clos des Princes

Twenty minutes on the train and you're in Paris. Here, behind wrought-iron gates in an elegant suburb, the French mansion sits in an exuberant town garden of pergolas, box bushes and mature trees. Your kind, attentive hosts – she an ex-English teacher, he with a passion for Prudhomme – give you the poet/philosopher's two-room first-floor suite; he lived here in 1902. Polished floorboards, pretty prints, choice antiques, decorative perfume bottles by a claw-footed tub – all dance to the 19th-century theme. Breakfast unveils gorgeous porcelain and delicious homemade muffins and jams.

Price	€95-€110.
Rooms	1 suite for 2 with separate bath. Sofabed available for children.
Meals	Restaurant 400m.
Closed	Mid-July to August.
Directions	From Paris Périphérique, exit Porte d'Orléans onto N20; A86 after Bourg la Reine to Versailles; exit 28 for Châtenay Malabry; over at Salvador Allende r'bout; right at 2nd r'bout; house on left.

Christine & Éric Duprez
60 avene Jean Jaurès, 92290 Châtenay Malabry

Tel   +33 (0)1 46 61 94 49

Villa Mansart

Wind your way up the handsome staircase and nudge open the attic door. The guest sitting room has sunny walls and ethnic rugs on pristine floors. Slim, arched bedrooms are blue or vanilla-and-orange with family furniture and windows that peep over the rooftops. Breakfast on fresh fruit and mini-pastries in an elegant dining room or on the terrace. Marble steps, rescued from a local demolition, sweep down to a huge, immaculate lawn; a curtain of trees shields you from the suburbs. All is peace and calm yet only 20 minutes from the centre of Paris.

Price	€88. Singles €70. Triple €118.
Rooms	2: 1 double, 1 triple. Extra single bed in sitting room.
Meals	Restaurants nearby.
Closed	Rarely.
Directions	From Paris A4 exit 5 for Pont de Nogent; at exit keep left, don't take tunnel; along viaduct; at 2nd lights under bridge; Ave. L. Rollin for Le Perreux centre; next lights straight on; 2nd left 200m.

Françoise Marcoz
9 allée Victor Basch, 94170 Le Perreux sur Marne

Tel	+33 (0)1 48 72 91 88
Web	www.villamansart.com

Paris Riverside

Your own cottage with a bushy bird-filled garden, the magnificent Marne flowing broad, tree-lined walks, boating, the little town shops – and Paris a short hop on the train. Behind an 1890s gentleman's residence are two sweet and modest bedrooms with a superb shower room; the 1950s extension is a large bright living space warmed by a generous fireplace. The kitchen has everything, the top-quality convertible sofa is supremely comfortable. The owners, both musicians, are most attentive: toys in the cupboard if children are staying, advice, bikes to borrow. *German spoken.*

Price	From €700 per week.
Rooms	1 double, 1 twin, 1 sofabed; 1 shower room, separate wc.
Meals	Restaurant 500m.
Closed	Rarely.
Directions	Directions on booking. Station 3-minute walk, Paris 20 minutes by train.

Aurore & Olivier Doise
12 rue Jean Mermoz,
94210 La Varenne Saint Hilaire

Tel   +33 (0)1 48 89 34 47
Web   parisriverside.fr

Entry 92 Map 1

La Maison du Coteau

The climb is worth every puff: a hawk's eye view to the Eiffel Tower, space and freedom in an unusual setup. One of a delightful bunch of Burgundy-based owners will welcome you to this generous light-filled house, providing the wherewithal for you to do breakfast when you like among an intriguing mix of antique and modern, French and Asian pieces. The many-sofa'd salon opens wide to garden and sky, front rooms have colour and light, the suite at the back is snug for families, the big penthouse is sheer delight. Use your own fridge and the splendid kitchen for meals, borrow a DVD – it's so friendly.

Price	€138–€220. Weekly rates available.
Rooms	4 + 1: 2 doubles, 1 twin/double, 1 family room. 1 penthouse with kitchen & terrace for 2-4 (double & bunks).
Meals	Restaurants nearby.
Closed	Never.
Directions	From A6 exit Arcueil: map on booking. RER B Arcueil-Cachan. Bus: 186 (Porte d'Italie).

Paris en Douce
94230 Cachan

Tel	+33 (0)3 80 49 60 04
Web	www.paris-en-douce.com

Entry 93 Map 1

Le Clos de la Rose

For birdwatchers and garden lovers (masses of roses, age-old trees), champagne buffs and cheese tasters (Brie on the doorstep, historic Provins nearby), this gorgeous green retreat from crazed Paris – cool, quiet, elegantly homely – has been restored with fine respect for an old flint house: limewash, wood, terracotta, a great gathering of books, paintings, prints. Both your hosts work from home and look after guests with care and intelligence. Bedrooms have pretty colours and mixed-style furniture, the adorable cottage (with kitchen) is ideal for a longer stay.

Price	€64–€138.
Rooms	2 + 1: 2 doubles. 1 cottage for 2 & kitchen.
Meals	Restaurant 5-minute drive.
Closed	Rarely.
Directions	From Paris A4 for Reims; exit 18 to La Ferté sous Jouarre; D407 for Montmirail; through woodland to Montapeine (6km from r'bout in La Ferté); D68 for St Ouen; 1.8 km right; 400m to black gate.

Martine & Jean-Paul Krebs
11 rue de la Source, L'Hermitière,
77750 St Cyr sur Morin

Tel	+33 (0)1 60 44 81 04
Web	www.clos-de-la-rose.com

Le Moulin de Saint Martin

Agnès, gentle, with artistic flair, and Bernard, gregarious, charming, convivial… together they have created a delectable B&B. The old mill is on an island encircled by Corot's Grand Morin river; lovely old willows lap the water, the pretty villages of Le Voulangis and Crécy lie beyond. A warm sober elegance prevails: there are 17th-century floorboards topped by oriental rugs; Asian antiques and art in gilt frames; cherry-red toile and snowy bed linen; terraces for summer views; log fires for nights in. Disneyland Paris, a world away, is a short drive; fine châteaux beckon. *Minimum stay two nights.*

Price	€65–€70.
Rooms	2: 1 double, 1 twin/double.
Meals	Dinner €20. Wine €15.
Closed	Rarely.
Directions	From Paris A4 for Metz, exit 16 for Crécy; 3rd lights right; through Crécy for Voulangis & Tigeaux. Leaving Crécy left, Le Moulin 200m, signed. Ring bell.

Bernard & Agnès Gourbaud
7 rue de Saint Martin, Voulangis,
77580 Crécy la Chapelle

Entry 95 Map 1

Tel   +33 (0)1 64 63 69 90

Manoir de Beaumarchais

It's charmingly bourgeois, and the welcome is warmly French. The house is a fascinating architectural cuckoo, an 'Anglo-Norman' face concealing an unspoilt 1920s interior with great arched windows and crested tiles. All is elegant, comfortable, beautifully furnished. Views are of stretching pastures. Your suite, as untouched as the aqua-panelled salon, is pretty, intimate and stylish, with a boudoir sitting room in the tower. Big breakfasts appear at the long dining table where, in good English, your retired hosts enjoy telling the history of grandfather's hunting lodge (they still organise shoots).

Price	€150.
Rooms	1 suite.
Meals	Restaurants nearby.
Closed	Rarely.
Directions	A4 to Metz exit 13 to Villeneuve le Comte; right opp. church D96 for Tournan; thro' Neufmoutiers, right opp. church, cont. 250m on D96; 1st left small road for Beaumarchais 1.5km; gates on left.

Nathalie & Michael Mavrinac
77610 Les Chapelles Bourbon

Tel	+33 (0)1 64 07 11 08
Web	www.beaumarchais.eu

Entry 96 Map 1

Ferme de Vert St Père

Cereals and beets grow in wide fields and show-jumpers add elegance to the fine landscape. A generous farmyard surrounded by very lovely warm stone buildings encloses utter quiet and a genuine welcome from young hosts and labradors alike, out here where Monsieur's family has come hunting for 200 years. Family furniture (the 1900s ensemble is most intriguing) and planked floors in beautiful bedrooms, immaculate mod cons and a super living area for guests in a beamy outbuilding with open fire, sofa, kitchen and TV. Exceptional house and setting, and a Michelin-starred auberge in the village.

Price	€62. Apartments €96.
Rooms	1 + 2: 1 family room for 3. 2 apartments for 4.
Meals	Restaurant in village (check opening times).
Closed	Christmas.
Directions	From A5 exit 15 on N36 towards Meaux, 200m; 2nd right to Crisenoy after TGV bridge, thro' village for Tennis/Salle des Fêtes; 1.5km to farm.

Philippe & Jeanne Mauban
77390 Crisenoy

Tel	+33 (0)1 64 38 83 51
Web	vert.saint.pere.free.fr

L'Atalante

Cocooned behind the garden walls, one of two hideaways leads straight off the garden. The uncluttered, open-plan space is fresh and bright with its cool cream floors, nautical stripes and pale walls, and, with its curtained-off sitting area and fire, most inviting. Up under the eaves is a fresh two-bedroomed suite overlooking the beautiful peonies and pathways. Tinkle the ivories in the *salon de musique*, stretch out on the flower-freckled lawn. You can use the kitchenette if you want to be independent or join your charming, interested and interesting hosts for dinner. One of our favourites.

Price	€58.
Rooms	2 suites: 1 for 2-4, 1 for 2-5.
Meals	Dinner with wine, €22. Guest kitchen.
Closed	Rarely.
Directions	From A5 exit 17 on D210 for Provins 2km; right D133 1km; left for Gardeloup. Left to Grand Buisson.

Florence & Georges Manulelis
8 rue Grande du Buisson, 77148 Laval en Brie

Tel   +33 (0)1 60 96 34 73
Web   latalante.free.fr

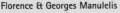

Château de Bourron

The early 17th-century château built on fortress foundations is hugely warm and inviting. Louis XV and his in-laws once met here and now it is owned by a charming young family. Inside is a feast of original Versailles parquet, oriental rugs, period pieces, exquisite fabrics and elegant tapestries. (Public rooms are reserved for receptions.) Guest rooms in the east wing are deep red and gold with marble bathrooms, gilt mirrors and Pierre Frey interiors: five-star stylishness in a château setting. On the first floor are a day room and a library. Outside, 80 acres of walled gardens and woodland, statues, chapel and pretty village.

Price	€180–€500.
Rooms	4 twins/doubles.
Meals	Breakfast €15. Dinner €38.
Closed	25 & 31 December.
Directions	Paris-Lyon A6 exit Fontainebleau. At 'obelisk' r'bout for Nemours-Montargis on N7; 8 km. Right for Villiers-sous-Grez, follow Bourron Marlotte Centre. Ring interphone at wooden gates in 2nd courtyard.

Entry 99 Map 1

Comte & Comtesse Guy de Cordon
14 bis rue du Maréchal Foch,
77780 Bourron Marlotte

Tel   +33 (0)1 64 78 39 39
Web   www.bourron.fr

Hôtel de Londres

Gaze on the Château de Fontainebleau, one of France's loveliest buildings, from your room in this 18th-century hostelry. The hotel has been in the family for three generations; Monsieur Philippe runs it quietly and considerately. In the sitting room, an 18th-century classical look; also rich colours and fine displays of flowers. The breakfast room has the feel of a small brasserie, and both rooms have views to Fontainebleau. Bedrooms are similarly classical in style – smart, spotless, traditional. A sense of timelessness pervades this peaceful place and you are well placed for exploring the hunting grounds of the kings.

Price	€110–€160. Suites €150–€180.
Rooms	15: 5 doubles, 2 triples, 1 single, 7 suites.
Meals	Breakfast €11.
Closed	23 December–9 January; 12-18 August.
Directions	A6 exit Fontainebleau for Château. Hotel opposite Château.

Philippe Colombier
1 place du Général de Gaulle,
77300 Fontainebleau

Tel	+33 (0)1 64 22 20 21
Web	www.hoteldelondres.com

Entry 100 Map 1

Château de Buno

The iron and limestone staircase is stunning and leads you to a suave sitting room on the landing with a white leather sofa on an ethnic rug. Off here, remarkable bedrooms lie. The original lighting installations, the glowing vintage pieces, the immaculately preserved bathrooms – Corinne, eager to please, fascinated by art and design, masterminds it all. All the rooms exude class: sweeps of parquet, a majestic Third Empire bed, a boudoir in the tower. Pastries and fresh fruits are laid on breakfast trays, candlelit dinners are delivered to your suite, and the swans and the well-stocked river float by serenely. *No credit cards.*

Price	€240–€270.
Rooms	5: 1 double, 4 suites.
Meals	Breakfast €15.
	Dinner, 4 courses, €40 (served in your room).
Closed	Rarely.
Directions	A6 Lyon, exit 13 onto D948. Milly la Foret 6.5km; D837 to Maisse; D449 at church to Gironville; 200m, left (in Petit-Gironville) to Buno Bonnevaux. On left, 400m after level crossing.

Corinne & Olivier Merciecca
Le Petit Gironville,
91720 Gironville sur Essonne

Entry 101 Map 1

Tel	+33 (0)1 64 99 35 25
Web	www.chateaudebuno.fr

Le Logis d'Arnières

Several centuries shaped this old hunting lodge, then it was determinedly 'modernised' in the 1920s Art Deco style: high-windowed, fully-panelled dining room with extraordinary dressers, fabulous bathroom fittings. It is exuberantly sober and shapely with Versailles parquet and fine fireplaces as well. Tae, from Chile, uses her perfect sense of style and colour to include these respected elements in her décor alongside richly baroque Chinese chairs and lots of South American pieces and paintings. Quiet spot, vast natural garden, joyous hosts, perfect for Chartres, Paris, Versailles.

Price	€80 for 2; €120 for 4.
Rooms	2 suites for 5.
Meals	Restaurant 200m.
Closed	Rarely.
Directions	From Paris A10 exit 10 to toll gate, right after toll; right again on D27 to St Cyr; continue for Arpajon; 1st house on left.

Claude & Tae Dabasse
1 rue du Pont-Rué,
91410 St Cyr sous Dourdan

Tel	+33 (0)1 64 59 14 89
Web	www.dabasse.com/arniere

À l'Ombre Bleue

Leave the willows to weep over the village pond, pass through the high gate into a wee sheltered paradise and a full coddle: the prettiest rooms with masses of old pieces, dolls, books, pictures to intrigue you, a chirruping garden with two rescue dogs to play with, the most caring hostess to provide an exceptional brunch, and dinner if you want (she teaches cookery and sources locally: it's delicious). The miniature garden-house is a lovers' dream: tiny salon downstairs, bedroom sporting superb bath up. Fulsome towels, extras of all sorts: charming, chatty Catherine thinks of everything.

Price	€65–€85.
Rooms	3: 1 double, 1 twin; 1 double in garden-house.
Meals	Dinner €22, including aperitif & wine. Light supper €14.
Closed	Rarely.
Directions	From Paris A13 exit 8 on A12; 1st exit N12 W 35km; left D983 16km to Faverolles; left D152/80 for Gazeran 5km; right D71 to stop sign; right; gate opposite village pond. Paris 45 minutes by train.

Entry 103 Map 1

Catherine Forget-Pépin
22 rue de la Mare, Les Patis,
78125 Mittainville

Tel	+33 (0)1 34 85 04 73
Web	www.alombrebleue.fr

Domaine des Basses Masures

The Rambouillet forest encircles this hamlet and the house is an old stables: long, low and stone-fronted, built in 1725. Madame does B&B at one end; the gîte is at the other. Bedrooms, carpeted, cosy and up under the eaves, have roof windows, new beds dressed in crisp cotton and fat pillows. In the sitting room there's a sofa that opens to a bed, a big oriental rug, modern wicker armchairs, an open fireplace. The kitchen, more functional than aesthetic, has a dining table and is well equipped; it leads into the garden, with outdoor furniture. Versailles is 20 minutes, Paris 45 and there's excellent walking from the door.

Price	€750 per week.
Rooms	1 double, 1 triple; 2 bathrooms.
Meals	Restaurants nearby.
Closed	Never.
Directions	Directions on booking.

Madame Walburg de Vernisy
13 rue des Basses Masures,
78125 Poigny la Forêt

Tel +33 (0)1 34 84 73 44
Web www.domaine-des-basses-masures.com

Entry 104 Map 1

Saint Laurent

Slow-paced medieval Monfort L'Amaury, 45 minutes from Paris, has 16th-century cobblestone paving, a Ravel festival in October and this superb private home built under Henri IV at the beginning of the 17th century. Old rafters reign in some bedrooms, the exposed beamed ceiling in the breakfast room is splendid and skilful carpentry is evident in the light oak used in the panelling, headboards and cupboards. Ground-floor rooms have private terraces looking out on the lawn where Madame Delabarre puts out fine summer chairs under the linden trees. There is a big accent on a full breakfast here which includes ham, eggs and cheese.

Price	€99-€199.
Rooms	18: 12 doubles, 3 twins, 3 suites.
Meals	Breakfast €12 (€8 on weekends). Restaurants within walking distance.
Closed	1-23 August.
Directions	From Paris, A13, A12, N12 towards Dreux then Monfort L'Amaury. In Monfort, thro' gates for car park.

Madame Christiane Delabarre
2 place Lebreton, 78490 Monfort l'Amaury

Tel	+33 (0)1 34 57 06 66
Web	www.hotelsaint-laurent.com

L'Orangerie

In a garden full of roses, behind the busy avenue leading to the château, a mini Marie-Antoinette Trianon holds two little luxury flats. Arched windows light a pale living area where a modern sofa flanked by Louis XV chairs stands on new parquet. The bathroom is marble, the kitchen a gem, the mezzanine bedroom generously comfortable and everything is brand new – except the antiques. One flat has a fuchsia-flashed colour scheme, the other is in sober taupe. Two couples can easily share the terrace, breakfast is at the friendly café over the road, the lively owners are around in the evening. Most civilised. *Minimum stay two nights.*

Price	€120–€155. Apartments from €135 per day. Includes breakfast in café.
Rooms	1 + 2: 1 double. 2 apartments for 2 with kitchenette.
Meals	Restaurants 300m. Light supper available.
Closed	Rarely.
Directions	Paris A13 to Rouen; after 7km exit 5 for Versailles-Centre/Château. Left, then Bd Jardy; Bd du Général Pershing & Ave. des États-Unis. Ave. de St Cloud. Ave. Rockefeller. Ave. de Paris. No. 37 on left.

	Patricia White-Palacio
	37 avenue de Paris, 78000 Versailles
Tel	+33 (0)9 53 61 07 57

Entry 106 Map 1

Pavillon Henri IV

Dumas, Offenbach and Georges Sand stayed here; the Sun King was born in a room off the entrance hall. There's a fascinating mix of styles, too – Renaissance domed roof, Art Nouveau porch. The view sweeps across the valley of the Seine to Paris and La Défense. Relish them from the rooms, the restaurant, the terrace: feel on top of the world. Bedrooms have been undergoing a gradual and welcome transformation, from classic sobriety to luxurious charm, while reception rooms are big and beautiful – white walls, parquet and rugs, gilded antiques, cornices, marble busts and sumptuous chandeliers. The dining is unquestionably lavish.

Price	€130–€250. Suites €290–€550.
Rooms	42: 40 twins/doubles, 2 suites.
Meals	Breakfast €16. Lunch €49 (not July/Aug). Dinner à la carte approx. €90.
Closed	Never.
Directions	A13 Paris-Rouen; exit St Germain en Laye on N186 to St Germain 'centre' via Ave Général Leclerc. At r'bout, over to Ave Gambetta; right at end onto Rue Thiers. On left.

Charles Eric Hoffmann
19-21 rue Thiers,
78100 Saint Germain en Laye
Tel   +33 (0)1 39 10 15 15
Web   www.pavillonhenri4.fr

7 rue Gustave Courbet

Behind the modest façade, on an upmarket housing estate, is a generous interior where Madame's paintings stand in pleasing contrast to elegant antiques and feminine furnishings. Picture windows let the garden in and the woods rise beyond. The larger guest room is soberly classic in blue, with a fur throw and big bathroom; the smaller one with skylight, books and bath across the landing is excellent value. Madame, charming and gracious, sings as well as she paints and enjoys cooking elegant regional dinners for attentive guests; she is very good company. Small, intimate, privileged, and so near Versailles.

Price	€55–€70.
Rooms	2: 1 double; 1 double with separate bath.
Meals	Dinner with wine, €18.
Closed	Rarely.
Directions	Paris A13 on A12 for St Quentin en Yvelines; exit N12 for Dreux; exit to Plaisir Centre; 1st exit off r'bout for Plaisir Les Gâtines, 1st left for 400m; right into Domaine des Gâtines; consult roadside plan.

Hélène Castelnau
Domaine des Gâtines, 78370 Plaisir

Tel   +33 (0)1 30 54 05 15

Cazaudehore – La Forestière

The rose-strewn 'English' garden is like an island in the great forest of St Germain. The first Cazaudehore built the restaurant in 1928, the second built the hotel in 1973, the third generation applies its imagination to receiving guests with elegant charm. The buildings are camouflaged among the greenery and summer eating is shaded under rose-red parasols; guests have the dining room with veranda to themselves (there are several seminar rooms). The chef's wine-tasting dinners and seasonal menus are renowned. Bedrooms are refined and unostentatious with good fabrics and furniture and much character. *Winter jazz dinners.*

Price	€205–€215. Suites €265–€285.
Rooms	30: 13 doubles, 12 twins, 5 suites.
Meals	Breakfast €20. Lunch & dinner with wine, €55–€70. À la carte €85. Child €23. Restaurant closed Mon all year and Sun evening November–March.
Closed	Never.
Directions	A13 for Rouen, exit 6 for St Germain en Laye on N186. N184 for Pontoise. Hotel on left 2.5km after château. RER A from Paris, then 5 mins by taxi.

Philippe Cazaudehore
1 avenue Kennedy,
78100 Saint Germain en Laye

Tel	+33 (0)1 39 10 38 38
Web	www.cazaudehore.fr

Les Colombes

On the doorstep of Paris, in the grounds of a royal château, surrounded by quiet tree-lined residential avenues, it's a trot from an atmospheric racecourse, almost on the banks of the Seine, with forest walks, good restaurants, efficient trains to and from Paris, impeccable, harmonious rooms, table d'hôtes and a deeply pretty garden to relax in. What Les Colombes lacks in old stones it makes up for in a welcome steeped in traditional hospitality – and that includes generous breakfasts, home-grown fruit and veg at dinner – and glowing antiques. Courteous, caring French hosts and great value.

Price	€75–€82.
Rooms	3: 2 doubles, 1 twin.
Meals	Dinner with wine, €35.
Closed	Rarely.
Directions	A15 exit 5 D392 thro' Cormeilles en P; right D121 to Sartrouville; right D308/Ave. Maurice Berteaux to Maisons-Laffitte; at château r'bout, 2nd right Ave. Carnot; over 3 x-roads to Ave. Béranger. Paris 15 minutes by train.

Irène & Jacques James
21 avenue Béranger,
78600 Maisons Laffitte

Tel	+33 (0)1 39 62 82 48
Web	perso.orange.fr/les-colombes

Entry 110 Map 1

Château d'Hazeville

Utterly original, a meld of brimming creativity and scholarship, Hazeville dazzles. Your artist host uses his fine château-farm, dated 1400s to 1600s, as a living show of his talents: huge abstract paintings, hand-painted plates and tiles, a stunning 'Egyptian' reception room (and loos), and now photography. The old stables house hi-tech artisans. Beautifully finished guest rooms in the *pigeonnier* are deeply luxurious; generous breakfasts come on china hand-painted by Monsieur to match the wall covering; he also knows the secret treasures of the Vexin. *Children over 7 welcome. Hot-air ballooning possible.*

Price	€135.
Rooms	2: 1 double, 1 twin.
Meals	Restaurants within 5-10km.
Closed	Weekdays & school term time.
Directions	From Rouen N14 for Paris; 20km before Pontoise, at Magny en Vexin, right D983 to Arthies; left D81 thro' Enfer; château on left.

Guy & Monique Deneck
95420 Wy dit Joli Village

Tel   +33 (0)1 34 67 06 17

Hostellerie du Prieuré

An immaculate hotel in a beautiful medieval village. Bedrooms are decorated with a flourish and a theme, from boudoir chic to Eastern exotica, all have have Middle Eastern carpets, gorgeous textiles, crisp sheets. There's purple-walled 'Aladdin' with a Syrian table and lovely 'Coloniale' with a bamboo four-poster, Indochinese prints and magnificent long views – down the village street all the way to Paris (25 kilometres). Yves and Frédérique are a warmly professional couple who also run an exhuberantly decorated gourmet restaurant a couple of houses away. All this luxury on the edge of fine forest; take the bikes and explore.

Price	€115-€185.
Rooms	8: 2 doubles, 1 twin, 1 family room, 4 suites.
Meals	Breakfast €13. Lunch €35-€50 (not Mondays). Closed Sundays.
Closed	2 weeks mid-August.
Directions	From Paris A15 for Cergy Pontoise, exit 115 dir. Taverny; exit St Leu La Forêt, St Prix on D139; 2nd street on right at r'bout; St Prix Village D144; left at light dir. Chauvry D193.

Frédérique & Yves Farouze
74 rue Auguste Rey, 95390 Saint Prix

Tel	+33 (0)1 34 27 51 51
Web	www.hostelduprieure.com

La Forge

There's a riding school next door, tennis in the village, walks in the forest – and Paris 30 minutes by train. At the back of the château is an exquisite apartment for two. The owners, cultured, delightful, the parents of three boys, live in the orangery of their 17th-century domain; an old gate leads to their house and beautiful-beyond-words garden. Your apartment is in the semi-basement of the old forge where the paintwork glows and the furniture is elegant antique. There's a sofa, a bed dressed in fine linen and paintings everywhere. The kitchen is small, neat, uncomplicated, but there is an excellent restaurant down the road.

Price	€500–€600 per week for 2.
Rooms	1 double, 1 sofabed; 1 bathroom.
Meals	Restaurants nearby.
Closed	Rarely.
Directions	Directions on booking.
	Station 500m, Paris 30 minutes by train.

Marie de Biolley
95590 Presles

Tel   +33 (0)1 34 70 06 56

Hotel

Oise

Relais d'Aumale

In a little village, the forest of Chantilly on its doorstep, this multi-faceted hunting lodge has character and a dazzling collection of armagnac on the carved stone mantelpiece. The rich, red beamed lounge is alluring, the glassy dining room is airy and light, opening onto the terrace and garden. Breakfast is usually in the cosy, panelled room next to the bar and there is an extensive wine list to choose from to complement your regional dinner. Bedrooms are comfortable, with warm, soft colours and fabrics, good bathrooms and double glazing. The Hofheinz's have created a relaxed and friendly atmosphere.

Price	€130–€156. Suites €190–€290.
Rooms	24: 22 twins/doubles. Petite Maison: 2 suites for 4.
Meals	Breakfast €14. Lunch €28–€36. Dinner from €44. Wine list €20–€30.
Closed	Christmas & New Year.
Directions	From Paris A1 for Lille, exit 7 onto N17 to Chantilly for 4km; left after La Chapelle en Serval onto D924a towards Montgrésin; signed in village.

Monsieur & Madame Hofheinz
37 place des Fêtes Montgrésin,
60560 Orry La Ville

Tel   +33 (0)3 44 54 61 31
Web   www.relais-aumale.fr

Entry 114 Map 1

Ferme de La Canardière

Forty kilometres north of Paris sits a house of classic 18th-century stamp. Polished limestone floors lead to an airy sitting room with leather sofas and huge stone fireplace. Tucked in one corner are two big bright bedrooms that lead directly onto a terrace, lawn and pool. A draped bedhead is partnered by splendid horsy curtains and posters. The twin – rich blue covers, antique cherry tables – feels elegant and bathrooms, tiled from top to bottom in blue and white, are sybaritic. In the kitchen Sabine, smiling and generous and a professional cook, produces wonderful breakfasts. Why not book into her masterclass?

Price	€150. Singles €130. Extra bed €25.
Rooms	2: 1 double, 1 twin.
Meals	Breakfast included. Hosted dinner, 4 courses with wine, €30. Restaurants 10-min walk.
Closed	Never.
Directions	From Chantilly N16 for Creil. Leaving Chantilly, cross bridge, 1st left opp. 'Arc de Triomphe' on Rue Guilleminot to viaduct; straight on, house on right above road.

Sabine Choain
20 rue du Viaduc, 60500 Gouvieux-Chantilly

Tel	+33 (0)3 44 62 00 96
Web	www.fermecanardiere.com

General information

A good place to start is the Paris tourist office (www.parisinfo.com). Tickets to museums, Disneyland, city tours, even boat trips can be purchased online; the main office at 25 rue des Pyramides is open every day (times vary slightly depending on the time of year) and can be reached by RER (Auber, line A) or metro (Pyramides or Opéra).

Getting around Paris

The layout

Finding your way in Paris is easier if you know that:

- the city is divided into 20 districts known as arrondissements, laid out in a clockwise spiral pattern that starts at Place de la Concorde
- street numbering is based on the Seine – places on streets perpendicular to the river are numbered outwards from it, odds on the left of the street, evens on the right; places on streets parallel to the river are numbered as the river flows, east to west
- the Left Bank (Rive Gauche) is the south bank of the Seine, the Right Bank (Rive Droite) is the north bank.

The maps in this guide are not street maps, so bring or buy one of the pocket street atlases, and get an excellent map of the metro and bus lines free from any metro station.

Don't use your car – it will cost you a fortune in parking fees and in frustration looking for somewhere to leave it. Also, Paris is already dangerously polluted and there is no need to add to that. Instead use the wonderful public transport system, it is one of the best in the world.

Buses

Stay overground and use the bus; some routes are perfect tours of Paris and its monuments. The number 24 crosses the Seine twice and runs along the south (left) embankment between the bridges. The 88 takes you past Montparnasse and the postmodern architecture of the Place de Catalogne, then on through the residential 15th arrondissement to the high-rise buildings of the new Left Bank development called Front de Seine. The 95 goes from the Left Bank up to Montmartre. Other good routes are 30,

48, 58, 73, 82 and 90. A system of night buses is also in service, providing late clubbers and night workers with easier transportation routes.

Metro

You are never far from one of the 300-odd metro stations, with trains that run between 5.30am and about 1am. Many of the stations have been radically refurbished over recent years and are full of interest just in themselves.

RER

The Paris RER consists of five express commuter trains that travel within Paris and the greater Paris region (unlike the

metro, which stops just outside the city limits). If you travel further than your ticket or pass allows you can be fined, so do make sure your pass covers the zones you need for your whole journey.

Batobus (Boatbus)

Not the speediest way to travel, but great fun and with lots to see, the boatbus uses the great watery road through the middle of Paris to take you, in eight stops, from the Eiffel Tower to the Hôtel de Ville and on to the Jardin des Plantes. Get off and on when you want; tickets can be bought for one or two days.

Bicycles

Vélib', the public bike rental programme, has been so popular since its launch in 2007 that there are now almost 20,000 bikes across the city with roughly one bike station every 300m. Maps of station locations are available at kiosks across the city. For more information go to www.velib.paris.fr.

Airport buses

Orlybus runs between Orly Airport and Place Denfert-Rochereau, 14th arrondissement, every 20 minutes. Roissybus is between Charles-de-Gaulle Airport and Opéra, 9th arrondissement. Air France buses, which run every 30 minutes, go between Charles-de-Gaulle Airport and Étoile, Porte Maillot or Montparnasse, and Gare de Lyon; or Orly Airport and Invalides or Montparnasse.

Museums

The Louvre, open 9am to 6pm (closed Tuesday), is free on the first Sunday in the month, as are all the national museums. Late nights are Wednesday and Friday till 10pm. A queue-beating tip: when the queue at the pyramid looks to be 24 hours long, face the Tuileries, your back to the pyramid, and to your left and right, next to the angels, are stairs to the underground entrance, which usually has much shorter queues. If arriving by metro, get off at the Palais Royal-Musée du Louvre station and use the entrance signposted directly from the platform.

As part of a new cultural policy, the permanent collections of fifteen other national museums in Paris can now be visited for no charge.

Food markets

Visit the food markets of Paris, soak up the feel of daily life here, even buy some of the ingredients that make it what it is. Covered markets may be in superb 19th-century iron-and-glass buildings. Some street markets consist of temporary stands set up two or three days a week, others are on pedestrian streets where the permanent shops simply extend their space onto the pavements. They are always colourful, lively and full of temptations (plus a few pickpockets) among their amazingly crafted mountains of fruit and veg. Look for stalls labelled *maraîcher*; they are market gardeners bringing good food direct from producer to end user. The last half hour before closing time on Sundays – midday or 1pm – can be rich in irresistible 'finishing up' offers.

Two of the larger covered markets (closed on Mondays) are:

• Marché Saint Germain, 6th (metro St Germain des Prés) – expensive but very good on fish and fresh vegetables; has an excellent Greek stall with delicious picnic ingredients

• Marché Saint Quentin, 10th (metro Gare de l'Est) – this magnificent 19th-century iron polygon has a variety of stalls including Portuguese, Italian and Kosher specialities, hardware and cobbling shops, excellent cheese, vegetable, fish and charcuterie and a café in the middle.

One of the most popular organic markets can be found on Boulevard Raspail, 6th arrondissement, every Sunday.

Photo: © Paris Tourist Office; Amélie Dupont

Walks

The two islands, Cité and St Louis, are good wandering areas. Guided walks, in French, are listed every week in *Pariscope* (a French-language magazine, available from any kiosk); English walking tours are available from www.paris-walks.com. Here are a few of our other suggestions:

1. See the permanent open-air sculpture garden along the river west of the Gare d'Austerlitz below Quai Saint Bernard. On warm evenings, each little riverside bay of this garden is given over to a type of music or dance: salsa, tango, folk dancing, many more – come and join in. Lots of lovely places with watery vistas; picnic on the grass and watch the boats float by. At the end, cross over to Île Saint Louis and walk along by those elegant 17th-century apartment buildings, built for the high-born of their day and still very select places to live. Take the Pont Saint Louis across to the Île de la Cité and the little garden below the east end of Notre Dame – don't miss the memorial to the Jewish deportees at the very eastern point of the garden. Walk west along the cathedral, gazing up at the stone miracles overhead, across the square past the hospital that is still known by its medieval name of God's Hostel (Hôtel Dieu) and right for a brief spell in all that traffic until you reach the Flower Market (a bird market on Sundays), which feels like a slice of tropical jungle adrift in northern Europe. And here is the Cité metro station with its original Guimard entrance, whence you can go north or south as you wish.

2. As well as containing world-famous examples of national building styles, built between the 1920s and the 1950s

to house foreign and French students in an ideal of harmony and international understanding, the Cité Universitaire has a vast 40-hectare park, so visitors can combine culture and fresh(er) air. The French architect Le Corbusier built the Swiss pavilion and also worked on the Brazilian pavilion. The new tram line passes just in front of the main campus area.

3. Wandering perpendicular to the Seine (one stretch is in a tunnel), the deliciously immobile, once old-fashioned Canal Saint Martin – now super-trendy with bistros, boutiques and cafes in every corner – was condemned to death by concrete in the 1970s, but good sense has prevailed. It is a stretch of tree-lined water where working and pleasure barges climb up and down the nine locks; Sunday afternoons are no-traffic times on the roads alongside and walking northwards is most enjoyable, ending with the treat of a good film and café on the banks of the Bassin de la Villette. Canal trips inside Paris or out into the countryside along the River Marne or the Canal de l'Ourcq are organised by Canauxrama, based at Bassin de la Villette.

Paris has many gardens, too. One of the most beautiful is Bagatelle, in the Bois de Boulogne (bus 43 from Gare St Lazare to Place de Bagatelle, or metro Porte Maillot). Renowned for its roses – old classics in a formal garden, hardy landscape roses in wilder settings – Bagatelle also has thousands of bulbs in spring and a huge variety of clematis, astonishing irises and masses of peonies in early summer.

Or visit the Père Lachaise garden-cemetery, Boulevard de Ménilmontant (metro Père Lachaise). This former Jesuit garden, a place of grand trees and lush fertility, was made a public cemetery by Napoleon 200 years ago; it is now, in effect, an open-air gallery of two centuries of funeral sculpture where visitors can wander among the mortal remains of the some of France's greatest musicians (Chopin, Rossini, Bizet), undying poets (Musset, Apollinaire, Nerval) and painters remembered in marble (Ingres, Delacroix, Pissarro); plus mainstream non-conformists such as Édith Piaf, Oscar Wilde and Jim Morrison.

If you have any comments on entries in this guide, please tell us. If you have a favourite place or a new discovery, please let us know about it. You can return this form to PAR, Sawday's, The Old Farmyard, Yanley Lane, Long Ashton, Bristol BS41 9LR, UK or visit www.sawdays.co.uk.

Existing entry

Property name: ─────────────────────────

Entry number: ───────────── Date of visit: ─────────────

New recommendation

Property name: ─────────────────────────

Address: ─────────────────────────

Tel/Email/Website: ─────────────────────────

Your comments

What did you like (or dislike) about this place? Were the people friendly? What was the location like? What sort of food did they serve?

─────────────────────────

─────────────────────────

─────────────────────────

Your details

Name: ─────────────────────────

Address: ─────────────────────────

───────────── Postcode: ─────────────

Tel: ───────────── Email: ─────────────

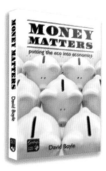

Money Matters
Putting the eco into economics
£6.99

This well-timed book will make you look at everything from your bank statements to the coins in your pocket in a whole new way. It holds the potential to change your life. In a world where the richest man is able to amass a fortune of over $50 billion, but over half the population of the planet live on less than $2 a day, this book discloses alternative and fairer ways. In his pithy and well argued style, author David Boyle sheds new light on our money system and exposes the inequality, greed and instability of the economies that dominate the world's wealth.

Do Humans Dream of Electric Cars?
Your journey to sustainable travel
£4.99

It is estimated that there are over 600 million motor vehicles being driven on the streets of the earth. This figure is expected to double in the next 30 years. But oil is running out and bio-fuels are no longer seen as a viable alternative to fossil fuels.

This guide provides a no-nonsense approach to sustainable travel and outlines the simple steps needed to achieve a low carbon future. It highlights innovative and imaginative schemes that are already working, such as car clubs and bike sharing and is published to coincide with the Sustrans's Change Your World Campaign 2009.

The Big Earth Book
Updated paperback edition
£12.99

This book explores environmental, economic and social ideas to save our planet. It helps us understand what is happening to the planet today, exposes the actions of corporations and the lack of action of governments, weighs up new technologies, and champions innovative and viable solutions.

What About China? £6.99
Answers to this and other awkward questions about climate change

A panel of experts gives clear, entertaining and informative answers arguing that the excuses we give to avoid reducing our carbon footprint and our personal impact on the earth are exactly that, excuses.

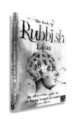

The Book of Rubbish Ideas £6.99

Every householder should have a copy of this guide to reducing household waste and stopping wasteful behaviour. Containing step-by-step projects, the book takes a top-down guided tour through the average family home.

Also available in the Fragile Earth series:

Ban the Bag A community action plan	£4.99
One Planet Living A guide to enjoying life on our one planet	£6.99
The Little Food Book An explosive account of the food we eat today	£6.99

To order any of the books in the Fragile Earth series call +44 (0)1275 395431 or visit www.fragile-earth.com

Have you enjoyed this book? Why not try one of the others in the Special Places series and get 35% discount on the RRP *

British Bed & Breakfast (Ed 14)	RRP £14.99	Offer price £9.75
British Bed & Breakfast for Garden Lovers (Ed 5)	RRP £14.99	Offer price £9.75
British Hotels & Inns (Ed 10)	RRP £14.99	Offer price £9.75
Devon & Cornwall (Ed 1)	RRP £ 9.99	Offer price £6.50
Scotland (Ed 1)	RRP £ 9.99	Offer price £6.50
Pubs & Inns of England & Wales (Ed 6)	RRP £15.99	Offer price £10.40
Ireland (Ed 7)	RRP £12.99	Offer price £8.45
French Bed & Breakfast (Ed 11)	RRP £15.99	Offer price £10.40
French Holiday Homes (Ed 4)	RRP £14.99	Offer price £9.75
French Hotels & Châteaux (Ed 5)	RRP £14.99	Offer price £9.75
Italy (Ed 5)	RRP £14.99	Offer price £9.75
Spain (Ed 8)	RRP £14.99	Offer price £9.75
Portugal (Ed 4)	RRP £11.99	Offer price £7.80
Croatia (Ed 1)	RRP £11.99	Offer price £7.80
India (Ed 2)	RRP £11.99	Offer price £7.80
Green Europe (Ed 1)	RRP £11.99	Offer price £7.80
Green Places to stay (Ed 1)	RRP £13.99	Offer price £9.10
Go Slow England	RRP £19.99	Offer price £13.00
Go Slow Italy	RRP £19.99	Offer price £13.00

*postage and packing is added to each order

To order at the Reader's Discount price simply phone +44 (0)1275 395431 and quote 'Reader Discount PAR'